WIDE LOAD [BRED LAST]
A House Moved

A HOUSE MOVED
[HUSFLYTTNINGAR]

WIDE LOAD [BRED LAST]
A House Moved

Tonia Carless   Robin Serjeant   paula roush

James Benedict Brown   Matthew Hynam

A HOUSE MOVED
[HUSFLYTTNINGAR]

Contents

Preface Un-building as spatial dialogue and moving buildings in Norrland — page 7

1. Uplift — page 11

Dialogue One: This is another Europe. A contextual discussion situating the house — page 35

2. The Move: Teg to Degernäs 10 Km — page 45

3. Settling. After the move to Degernäs — page 71

Dialogue Two: A very strange looking house and it appears to only lightly touch the ground. A discussion about the nature of the house, its interior and a small vision event — page 85

4. Digital Model — page 95

Essay: Moving materials and ways of life — page 106

Essay: A house moved [Husflyttningar] — page 122

WIDE LOAD
[BRED LAST]

5. Moving inside Degernäs — page 139

6. Long load [Lång last] — page 159

7. Sinking. Other lives of the cabin [Stuga] demolition — page 175

Dialogue Three: What is this mound? A Discussion about the demolition of cabins at lake Nydala, their relation to the moving house and a small vision event — page 187

8. Sloyd model and other representations — page 197

9. Husflyttningar as culture — page 233

10. Ep[a]log event — page 251

Volunteers Poster — page 257

Acknowledgements — page 260

Colophon — page 264

A HOUSE MOVED
[HUSFLYTTNINGAR]

Preface

UN-BUILDING AS SPATIAL DIALOGUE AND MOVING BUILDINGS IN NORRLAND

Tonia Carless + Robin Serjeant

A HOUSE MOVED
[HUSFLYTTNINGAR]

This book sets out a series of translations of form and corresponding thinking around an un-building project in the city of Umeå Västerbotten Northern Sweden in 2021 and 2022.

The term translations implies a shift from one form to another, a changing state and corresponding ideas about these shifts in the understanding and knowledge around both a moved house and the redevelopment and reconfiguration of space in and around Umeå. It is forged from a series of readings and moments using film, photography, drawing, installation, projection and writings of history and construction of particular vernacular dwellings in the region. 'Un-building' is used as a spatial dialogue and its origins are influenced through consideration of the work of Gordon Matta-Clarke (*Splitting* 1972)[1], Jeremy Deller (*It Is What It Is. Baghdad On tour* 2007)[2] and Rachel Whiteread (*House* 1993)[3].

In making and remaking buildings some of the questions considered are: What was there before it was built? How did this space come to be here? How was the space thought about before the building? What is the space beneath at the moment it is to be moved? What is there once the building has been moved? How has the space beneath changed when the building is transported?

It is not an open-ended investigation into what might be the known and unknown, but it is looking at specific moments and phenomena and these are particular to both the place of Umeå, in Northern Sweden and the space of the moving house. One proposal put forward by the research is that the conditions of applying loads onto timber and ground, which is a fundamental material consideration here, need to be investigated through the pressing of things into timber itself.

The form of the book has been developed as a collaborative work and is structured around concepts of geological movement experienced in northern Sweden of uplift [4]. It considers how architecture is attached to landscape through the process of moving buildings and the idea of the unstable and non-fixed that this implies through concepts of settling (settlement) of built form and the simultaneous capacity of sinking and collapse into the ground of both settlement and built form due to prevailing economic, social and or environmental conditions.

The space of the book, of necessity, uses representation as a form of research. It does this through image and text and both have a non-academic aspect to their field of investigation. The dialogue format is intended as a non-academic writing, as a more immediate, notational and open frame of thinking about the subject matter. It is inserted to give insight into some of the socio- spatial arrangements of moving from one terrain to another as well as the setting up of image projections and small vision events.

The book prefigures and records events connected to moving houses in the region. Although the images and text have a chronological order in part, there is the idea of a continuous feedback loop where text and image might be read and re read to further develop knowledge in the subject matter. The book itself has an architectural form through its assembled texts, spaces and images.

1.UPLIFT

1. UPLIFT

Magnus Martensson of Nya Töre Husflyttningar AB has physically moved over 400 buildings using traditional methods of lifting up the buildings.

1. UPLIFT

Uplift considers the house before the move. It is the state of the house at first sight, at 9 Lansmansvagan, Teg, in the city of Umeå, Västerbotten, Northern Sweden (Norrland) after its first uplift of 70 tonnes of built house and furnishings, wrenched from the ground, brick and stone chimney and foundations removed and the house supported on timber stacks (cribs) and waiting for transportation to Degernäs. The initial investigation and seeking out of the house was through an interest in the notion of an architecture of de-growth through relocation and the tradition of moving buildings in the region.

It also describes the first encounter with the house mover Magnus Martensson of Nya Töre Husflyttningar AB, who has physically moved over 400 buildings using traditional methods of lifting up the building to rest on timber baulks before transportation. This house move was undertaken by three men and assisting Magnus were Erik and Albert the driver.

The research analyses the specific (local) context of uneven development, it recognizes that the land beneath the house has a greater financial value to be released through this moving. The lifted house, resting and waiting, seemed to offer a potential for methods of investigating new knowledge using Västerbotten and Umeå's particular histories of settlement (the making and un-making of space) to frame an understanding and an approach to an embedded social sustainability. The historic land division map of 1923 shows the land, house and its barn in alignment. At the point of uplift its

1.UPLIFT

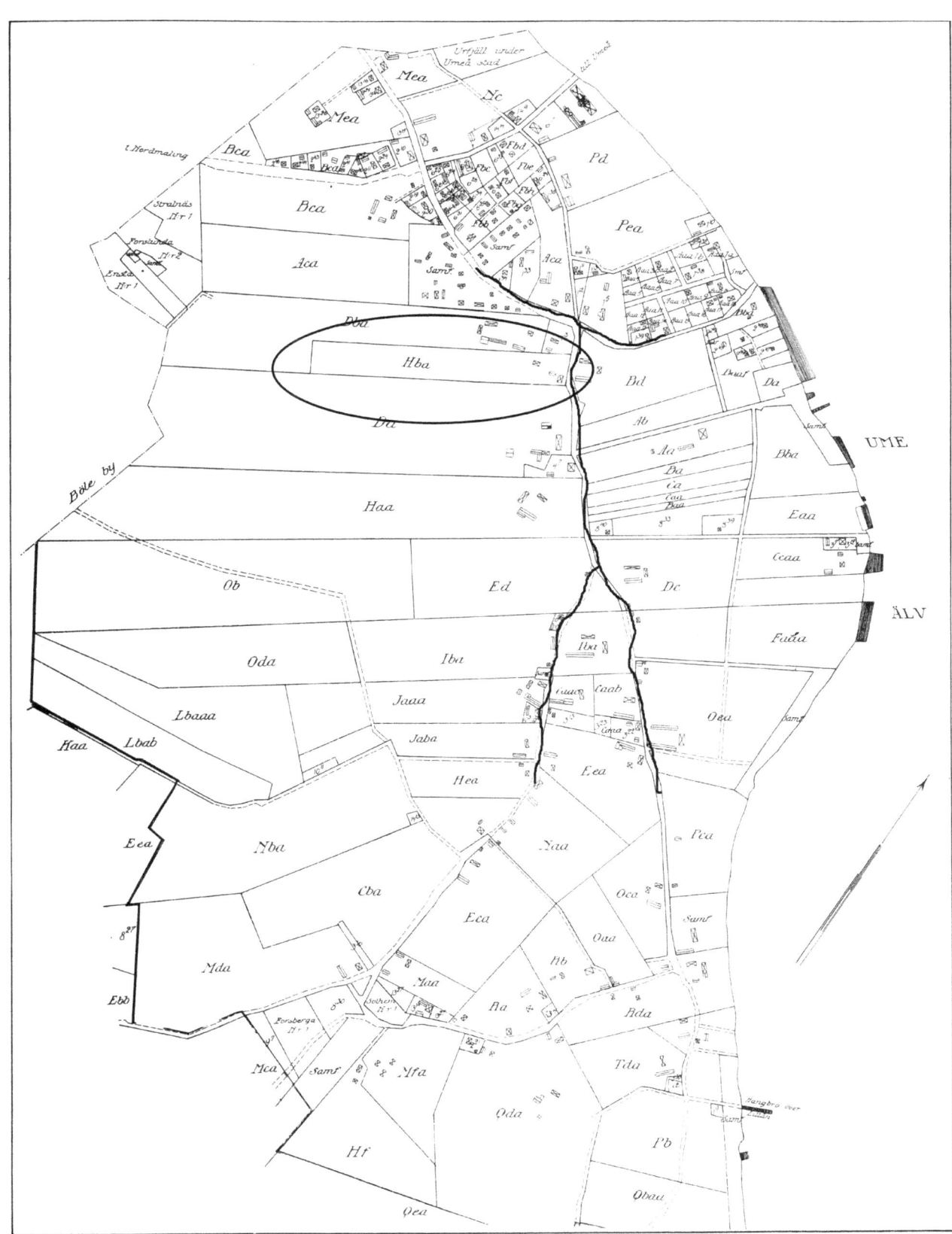

Karta över viss del av Tegs och Öns skifteslag uti Umeå socken från laga skifteskartan utdragen samt kompletterad år 1923 av Paul Wagenius, överlantmätare.

Local History Studies Umeå Public Library

1.UPLIFT

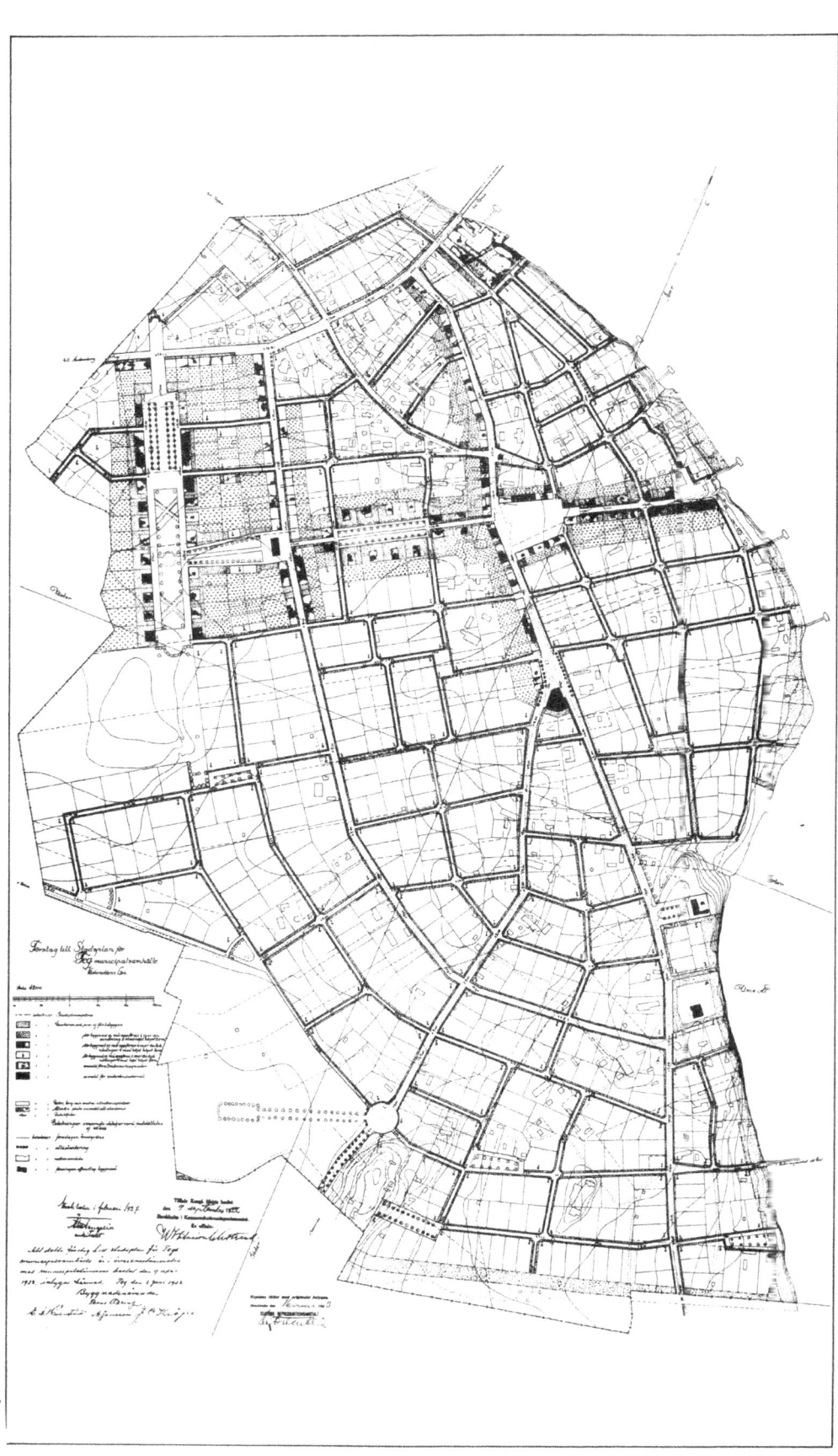

Stadsplan för Tegs municipalsamhälle upprättad i februari 1927 av arkitekt Åke Tengelin, Stockholm, fastställd den 9/9 1932.

Local History Studies Umeå Public Library

orientation is out of line with the more contemporary urban grid. It was one of the few remaining historic houses in this part of the city. While the project forms a specific and local analysis it is used here to frame an approach and methodology that could be extended to ask questions about the wider, global context of settlement and reconfiguration of space

The research is centred on how and why the moving was made possible and what processes were involved. On seeing the house and its garden after the uplift in April 2021 new questions arose regarding the values ascribed to historic context in the city of Umeå, about how the house was selected for moving and what process of regulation might be involved. Other questions arose about how in fact it was lifted, the structural conditions and forms of lifting, moving and support through very basic compressed and compressing timber stacks (cribs). The uplift seemed to offer an unseen condition between land and house and also a dynamic trajectory towards its new rural location beyond the city. The idea that it was to be moved by only two men and one driver also formed a sense of wonder about the methods and processes.

The idea of site safety seemed counter to conditions known from current British construction sites. The openness of its condition as well as the Swedish notion that everyone will take personal responsibility for their own safety were tangible. The Swedish notion of open accessibility to land through Allemansrätten[5] also formed part of this condition, allowing for a particular approach to both territory and site. This concept was also understood within the critical framework that

1.UPLIFT

has allowed for the colonisation
of much of the land in Umeå,
both by the University and others
(Stens and Sandstrom: 2014)⁶

[1] Gordon Matta-Clark (1974) Film *Splitting* Whitney Museum of American Art https://whitney.org/collection/works/12740 (Accessed March 2022)

[2] Jeremy Deller (2009) Film *It is What it is Baghdad on tour* https://www.jeremydeller.org/ItIsWhatItIs/ItIsWhatItIs_Video.php (Accessed March 2022)

[3] Rachel Whiteread (1993-94) Sculpture https://www.artangel.org.uk/project/house/ (Accessed March 2022)

[4] Reference Geological uplift of the region

[5] The freedom to roam or 'everyman's right' granted by the Constitution of Sweden amended 1994 https://en.wikipedia.org/wiki/Freedom_to_roam#Sweden (Accessed May 2022)

[6] Stens, Anna and Sandstrom, Camilla. (2014) *Allemanstratten in Sweden: A Resistant Custom*, Umeå University

1.UPLIFT

1.UPLIFT

1. UPLIFT

1.UPLIFT

1.UPLIFT

1.UPLIFT

1.UPLIFT

1.UPLIFT

1.UPLIFT

1.UPLIFT

1.UPLIFT

1.UPLIFT

1.UPLIFT

1.UPLIFT

1.UPLIFT

1.UPLIFT

1.UPLIFT

DIALOGUE ONE

Dialogue One
This is
another
Europe.
A contextual
discussion
situating
the house

Tonia Carless – Robin Serjeant

DIALOGUE ONE

Dialogue 1. This is another Europe
A contextual discussion situating the house.

digital models of Brabazon hangars
Greenland map — indigenous knowledge
Sami dwelling, back garden, Umeå

There is a limited pallet of colours here red
and yellow of Sami hut and grey mainly — the
sky blue parts are so blue

Some of the cabins have collapsed since last
year and one is now tilting over. The depth of
snow must have been heavy

Watched "Nostalgia for the Light" about the
Atacama desert in Chile, it considers acts
of looking and acts of time marking and
remembering. Very moving in bringing together
astronomy, archaeology, and Pinochet state
terror victims.

Just listened to fascinating programme on
issue of digital memories, and the matter
of old news stories about individuals being
stored and accessible for years afterwards.

Today is grey and looks a bit Soviet outside
again. The gardens between some of the houses
behind are so lovely. They are more mature
and they are shared and very social spaces.
These here are less so with fences between and
the sheds forming privacy between. There are
snow bars? on the roofs to stop it sliding off
and part of the roof is some kind of crimped
metal. From this window and, of course,
the forest.

and pasting sections from: "Extractive
Violence on Indigenous Country", by Kristina
Sehlin MacNeil. She researched asymmetries of
power between state and corporations and

indigenous peoples, Arctic Circle and southern Australia

The light qualities here are amazing and out of the ordinary it would be good for looking across iron ore and mica surfaces

silver birch ....
everywhere.
reading earlier about 'Old Tjikko', Norway spruce, 9500 years old, identified by Umeå University.

farm and forest

frosty fisherman who refused English speaking. He was moving stuff to the new cabin on the lake side of the path. Now more acutely aware of abandoned nature of some of the cabins there, rather than them being boarded up for the winter

City edges - sounds good.

lists of abandoned settlements in Västerbotten. So far historical research regarding C19th.
Sure there is more recent information
- perhaps population statistics held by municipality?

Watching Västerbotten documentary of town where 15 year old girls drive chopped down Volvos at no more than 30 mph, as taxi drivers for a festival.
https://www.svtplay.se/video/27333929/epa

suggested as a reference:
https://en.wikipedia.org/wiki/Solitude_Trilogy

https://www.youtube.com/watch?v=szgnGV4hOKU

lyric ' nothing but flowers', talking heads

SVT article about the house and Anders

lack of fence around the object.
there should be steps and verandah
reindeer herding and territories
The exceptional status of reindeer husbandry
under Covid access to Sweden

the space under the raised house could be the
artefact, or imagine raised Bildmuseet, as the
source and form of the artefact, it suddenly
occurred to me that the space under the house
could be recorded as a photogrammetry model

thinking more about the space below the house,
to frame it more as a critique of
gentrification

The photogrammetry would require standing or
at least positioning under the house

if it were to be a shallow volume, possibly
a cast in addition to photogrammetry
projections?
The artefact as part of a wall perhaps,
modified, but the capture of the space between
the mobile building and the ground is a
stronger idea in
terms of space, territory, expropriation of
land and more.

underside photos
Thinking about this space as a 3d volume,
digital or otherwise.

looking up definitions of gentrification
https://www.svt.se/nyheter/lokalt/
Västerbotten/sa-har-hamnade-lenin-i-jorn

Jörn railway station

Jörn
Magnus

DIALOGUE ONE

EPA tractor

A house moving project was a first fascination on arriving here too, of the historic Sami house in Amir's garden

Lots of shots of the underside and spaces. The east side of it seems that the sand and ground might be unstable. Tomorrow they will move the trees so it will change

house and lorry

Did you find the inflating pillow?
Yes it was there, they may repair it. No one took things from the site and how much Magnus had left

Tools, straps, timbers and ply, lifting gear and more

The key is in the front door of the house
Some things have moved inside
It looks out over the forest
There is Umeå then nothing

There is Umeå then nothing

Rural
Everything is rural
Even the city

Forest and more forest?
The guide book described north Swedish coastal strip, as distinct to hinterland, up to Norwegian border.

Rough guide?
Already out of date
Even google maps can't keep up.
Speed of development…amazing
Like the house – here today...

DIALOGUE ONE

When drawing the route of the house move the digital map was so out of date

Just aware still of strangeness. I was comfortable with the landscape this evening as we drive out to the village. It was the first time. The pine trees felt familiar and not too scary and I imagined that I could live in a house in the village looking out onto the cow parsley
And the lupins
And even the pines

Heals and homeless
But the houses here are slippery
Across the ice and over the sea

The stones are cut on one side sometimes so worth only about 500 SEK then. The uncut side sits inwards where you don't see it- of course that knowledge lies in the space under the house

stones and wagon

The new position of the timber props — 'cribs' he said they are called in USA, and the herd of stones too

steels

It's like driving in the USA (hence all the big American cars). It's a slow driving and sense of open road, the road works are a sight to behold too. I found lots of strange landscapes, some reminiscent of Avonmouth with a massive Smurfit Kappa industrial plant.

the loss of attachment to nature and the land here which must be accelerating because of the internet. Of course, this happens everywhere but the size, scale and minimal occupation will have a significant impact in a place like

DIALOGUE ONE

this - further north more of course. It is
amazing and beautiful and scary all at the
same time. There was something more,
It's to do with the space away from work as
a summer holiday frame, where imagination
and thinking, being physically detached for
a duration, is important but still only a
generation away.

'To the north' carries more questions than I
realised earlier
It's also about equity of resources here
Not competition

Equity - including rights of passage?
Allemansrätten
and access to camping roaming (as long as
you're not Sami with a herd of reindeer)

Multi storey timber building Wondering
about Töre Husflyttningar moving it and the
possibilities of that and thinking about "ask
not how much your building costs but how much
it weighs" Buckminster Fuller I wonder also
where the timber comes from and what process
is required for lamination.

I am not comfortable with the idea of staying
here after the trip tonight. I thought that
I was getting used to it here but it is so
massive out there

But it's light and dawn is coming 23:02
It was so misty and felt like autumn

"Gustav Metzer using acid on nylon...."
American car, garden

The politics of intervening around Lake Nydala
will take time to register, and untangle, and
a two week project is not a suitable vehicle
for that.
The research and practice always looks at the
arrangement of power and ways to mark or

DIALOGUE ONE

intervene in the socially overlooked or socially appropriated.

cabin in the woods inhabited by an older person who uses a walking frame

summer/winter awaiting demolition
cabins and lake

I have just been excitedly scouring Länsmanvägen and Degernäs on google maps. On two sides it is snow and one side it is summer 2014, and the family are alive. The road in Degernäs is not traversable with my little yellow man

Can you capture this material? Otherwise, I presume that in time the material will be updated, and the family will disappear......

Lectures and projects could be given and made about the absence of the house perhaps? Also, there are questions about what then happens, and how to construct ideas of placing, and locating, and making exteriors and interiors. Is this a Radical Localism? What is not known and what is presumed (by professionals and commercial interests) for the production of things, space and buildings?

demolition of house

That house could have been saved and moved by Magnus and Erik, and the one next to it they are / were really beautiful
The smell of demolition is so wonderful it's plaster and sawdust. I miss building sites.

DIALOGUE ONE

2. THE MOVE

2. THE MOVE: TEG TO DEGERNÄS 10 KM

The six hour long, night time, public event.

2. THE MOVE

This section considers the space beneath the house as a form of conceptual and physical spatial extension. It's focus is on the Midsummer June 21, 2021 uplift and repositioning onto the low loader and the subsequent journey through and out of the city of Umeå to Degernäs. It considers in further detail house moving practices and histories. It records the process undertaken by Magnus Martensson and his assistant Erik of Nya Töre Husflyttningar, including consideration of their durational working knowledges of structure and load over time which is understood to be constituted by both physical knowledges and craft skills.

It documents the move of the six hour long, night time, public event, on the longest day of the year in a northern geographical terrain with near midnight sun.

2. THE MOVE

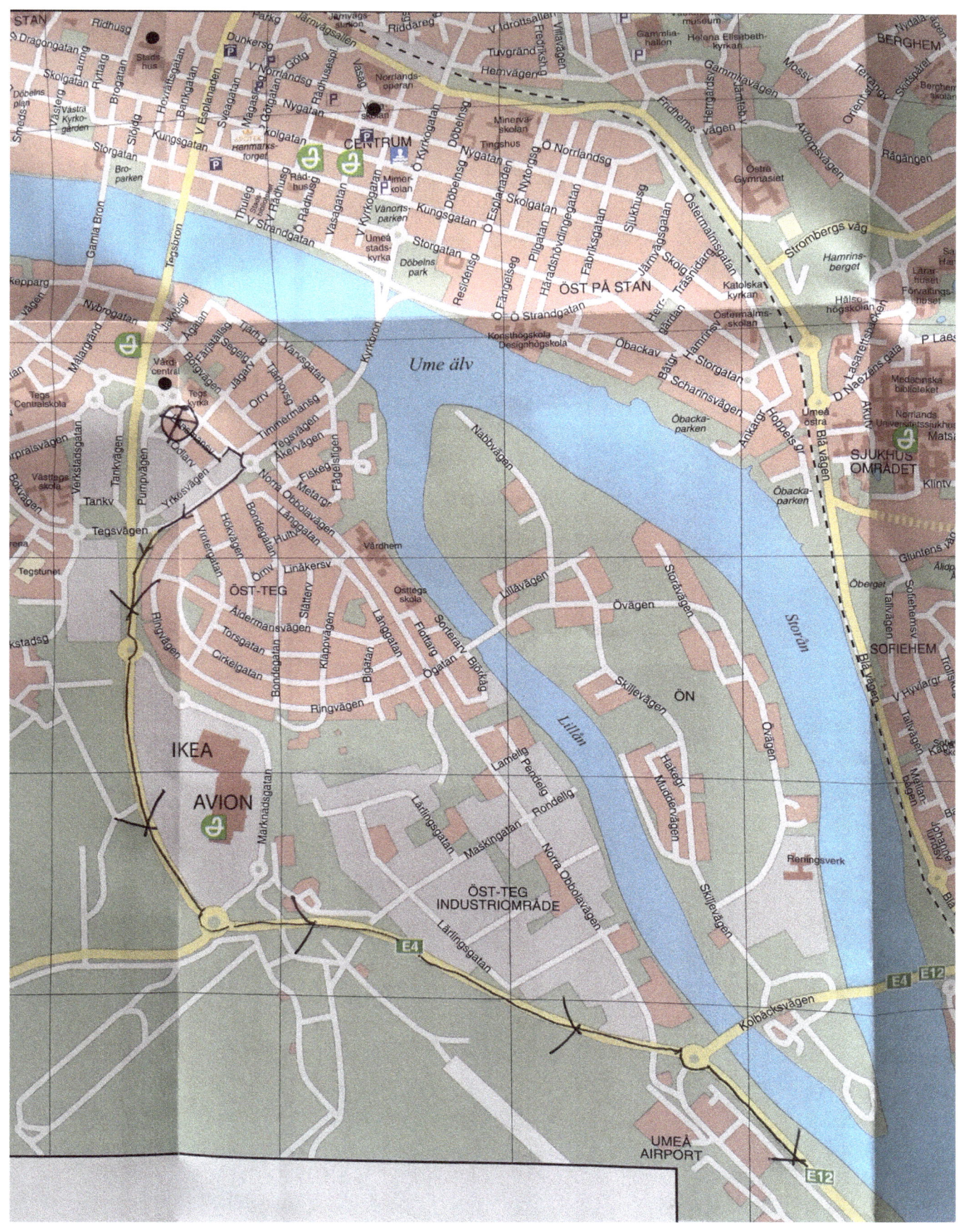

2. THE MOVE

2. THE MOVE

2. THE MOVE

2. THE MOVE

2. THE MOVE

2. THE MOVE

2. THE MOVE

2. THE MOVE

55

2. THE MOVE

2. THE MOVE

2. THE MOVE

2. THE MOVE

2. THE MOVE

2. THE MOVE

2. THE MOVE

2. THE MOVE

2. THE MOVE

2. THE MOVE

2. THE MOVE

2. THE MOVE

2. THE MOVE

2. THE MOVE

3. SETTLING AFTER THE MOVE TO DAGERNAS

3. SETTLING AFTER THE MOVE TO DEGERNÄS

The house has been relocated into a rural context. The timber cribs have been repositioned onto a concrete footing.

3. SETTLING AFTER THE MOVE TO DAGERNAS

The house has been relocated into a rural context, onto a made up tract of land from a forest clearance site. The timber cribs have been repositioned onto a concrete footing, the house on its steel framework is positioned onto the cribs and additional concrete block pillars. The distant views back to the city show glimpses of the Volvo plant beneath the house between house and land.
The house is lifted by six inflatable pillows positioned beneath and soap is used to free the steels from the timber base and underside of the house. Steels are removed and the house is lowered into place.
The foundation stones arrive on the site from Teg and are levered under the house, into position and fixed.

3. SETTLING AFTER THE MOVE TO DAGERNAS

3. SETTLING AFTER THE MOVE TO DAGERNAS

3. SETTLING AFTER THE MOVE TO DAGERNAS

3. SETTLING AFTER THE MOVE TO DAGERNAS

3. SETTLING AFTER THE MOVE TO DAGERNAS

3. SETTLING AFTER THE MOVE TO DAGERNAS

3. SETTLING AFTER THE MOVE TO DAGERNAS

3. SETTLING AFTER THE MOVE TO DAGERNAS

3. SETTLING AFTER THE MOVE TO DAGERNAS

3. SETTLING AFTER THE MOVE TO DAGERNAS

3. SETTLING AFTER THE MOVE TO DAGERNAS

DIALOGUE TWO

Dialogue Two
A very strange looking house and it appears to only lightly touch the ground.

A discussion about
the nature of the house,
its interior and a
small vision event

Tonia Carless + Robin Serjeant

Dialogue 2. a very strange looking house and it appears to only lightly touch the ground.

It's not Magnus because it was moved by a crane (the modern way)

The ideas-analysis is about the early stages of re-thinking, using Rachel Whiteread and Gordon Matta-Clark as coordinates, as a way to push for clarification of ideas and intent.

I also thought about the space between the house and the ground of the moving house while I was watching the dancing. About all of its moving processes and different components and making it, and the slivers of bark and those visible bark edges to the timber joists underneath the floor
of that house.
I would like to make that now, slowly, in slow time, in a cabin by a lake or the sea

Where do students go when they need to discuss images and objects, when they have prints or models or constructions? Where can they gather around a set of things (not screens) to discuss
and compare their work, or references? They need
to be around, beside, in front and behind things, to learn, to observe, to describe, more than ever now, after 18 months of intense flat screen gazing

Teg, after dark

I would like to hold a vigil for the house. We could ask Anders permission for this and think that some projection will be involved. At the

beginning of December could be a good time to
do it. We could invite students and some staff
and researchers maybe ... a small group

I was thinking about night time events in Umeå
and that if we were doing a procession, moving
the under house space, we could stick posters
up
https://www.svt.se/nyheter/lokalt/
Västerbotten/har-rivs-stugorna-vid-nydalasjon-
i-Umeå
Västterbotten Museum - the house reappears

I just had a realisation that images sent by
WhatsApp are not as well defined as if they are
sent by email. You cannot see the white marble
city which is the Volvo plant in that image in
the background and beyond the gap under the
house at Degernäs.
Dark photographs of the house please,
for a book chapter
It was solid ice. She came out of nursery
wielding her axe and broke some ice with it
but it was quite thick so it was hard to swim
- only dipping was possible with chunks of
floating ice

Still red car

Uncertain. The instability and un permanence
of ground and things. The fleetingness of human
constructions?
All things return to (saw)dust

dark house flyer

https://amp.svt.se/nyheter/lokalt/
Västerbotten/small-pa-tomtebo-nationella-
bombskyddet-har-sokt-av-platsen

This also made me feel very strange having
heard the blast

The new flyer.
The dark house image was intriguing,
but not funny.

We should be enjoying the contradictions and
strangeness of things, as part of actions
and thinking.

At Degarnäs and Teg, we must have laughter
and wonder, this is really important.

Video still

These signs are appearing everywhere and it's
gouging out my soul even though my attachment
here is slight and short lived, but it's
because of what it represents

Cabin demolitions

going into forest in minus 10, and snow, and
dawn/dusk.

timber stacks, which become a surface for
small projections?

And the photos of the Degarnäs void could be
projected and the other views of Degarnäs

The timber baulks, arranged vertically, as
they were arranged in the process of lifting,
and lifting off the house from the Teg ground?

Other ideas of height, of projecting upwards,
projecting at different levels,

And maybe the poles / screen could be replaced
by a regular portable digital screen so
nothing needs making, just arranging the
timbers and screen on top

Not sure of substance, scale, environment ...
Ice and river

Good to see the Teg site in dusk light.
The birds are impressive, in number and
freewheeling in the air above the snow.

The projections work well, windows on walls
and on windows
On small things and larger
Larger & larger
But fingers and phone battery stopped working
in 10 minutes

Teg night & Degarnäs snow

Is the height of the window cills what you
imagine they were and the upper floors too?

Maybe trestles?

Yes, it seems that windows are wrong. I am
working on the plan about how to use them.
I was wondering about how high the cills might
be so that the upper levels would require
significant constructions, if a projection
screen were to be set at the same height as
the upper floor windows.

The ground is too unsafe to do in the snow —
and there is the central hole

Are you thinking of cills for first floor
windows
at Degarnäs?
And replicating that height at Teg?

It's such a serious landscape and climate that
so much could go wrong. I try not to think
about it too much but it is there of course.
We have 2 days to put the project together
(together) Tuesday and Wednesday only. Making
the banner/s screens and selecting images

and ordering them and buying lamps/ candles.
I don't know even if I will make it out of
here for Christmas ... it only takes Covid or
another virus and one of us to be unwell and
it's all over... that's a bit overwhelming too

I am beginning to wonder at the strangeness of
this environment to those who have not grown
up in it or have at least been there for some
years.
Its visually unbalancing. And with extreme
cold perhaps it does seem hostile, even in
more familiar places

I went into the house next door (the
neighbours) this morning, I was so confused
and disorientated

There was a woman and her dog skiing on the
lake

I bought two LED candles and thought that
maybe we could have real ones outside the
house at the front like they do at the front
of shops

There is still much for to discuss as well,
including around the set of images, and where
they might appear.

Met office indicate snow Thurs and Friday. So
it is likely that Teg will be in snow.

Imagine how snow light changes the inside
spaces and surfaces
Notes photo

Interiors

The current divisions of images into folders
for projections:

A. Maps, drawings, aerial and panorama photos
of Degernäs
B. Teg - ready to move
C. Underside, stack, ground
D. Moving
E. Teg, site remains

There are too many images, if put it onto auto
run through, it will run too long in this cold

Using simple organising concepts to sequence
images in each folder.
Then a discussion about where to project the
different folders.

I was wondering about making projections onto
the space where the sawdust house was, and
into the cabins today

I am wondering where we can find a significant
pile of sawdust - saw mill? Or house being
reduced, though the snow cover might make it
invisible.

23 October A pile of 2020 snow covered by a
thick layer of sawdust to act as insulation
material to preserve snow through summer
temperatures of 30 plus degrees. The snow is
to be used for the cross-country ski track at
Nydala early in the following season

I heard it said that the Swedish and Umeå
Kommun tend to treat buildings as objects (for
historical or other study) rather than a more
contextual approach

Waiting for plane, and so started reviewing
'Teg to Degernäs' images.
The birch tree and leaning flag pole near the
site is really good!

bus stop etc.

London from above, lit up, was awe making.
Such a variety of lights, colours and shapes.
Digital weave in lights of huge complex carpet

cabins and snow

cabins in snow

wooden structures, in woods north west England

house cake

Preparation for a midwinter projection event
inside the moved house at Degernäs. Projecting
views from Teg onto the windows, central
chimney void and other interior spaces and
considerations of returning the house to Teg
as a series of public projections.

DIALOGUE TWO

4. DIGITAL MODEL

4. DIGITAL MODEL

Digital model made using Photogrammetry software and multiple photographs of the underside of the house.

4. DIGITAL MODEL

A digital model is made using Photogrammetry software and multiple photographs of the underside of the house at Teg and Degernäs. The model has some gaps, of missing information, where the centre of the underside is difficult to access, but also has some uneven representation where the interior is visible from below and beneath. It is possible to experience the house interior in part from an underground aspect. The model allows for the possibility of representing the space as a solid object with highly rendered photographic quality surfaces.

4. DIGITAL MODEL

4. DIGITAL MODEL

4. DIGITAL MODEL

4. DIGITAL MODEL

4. DIGITAL MODEL

101

4. DIGITAL MODEL

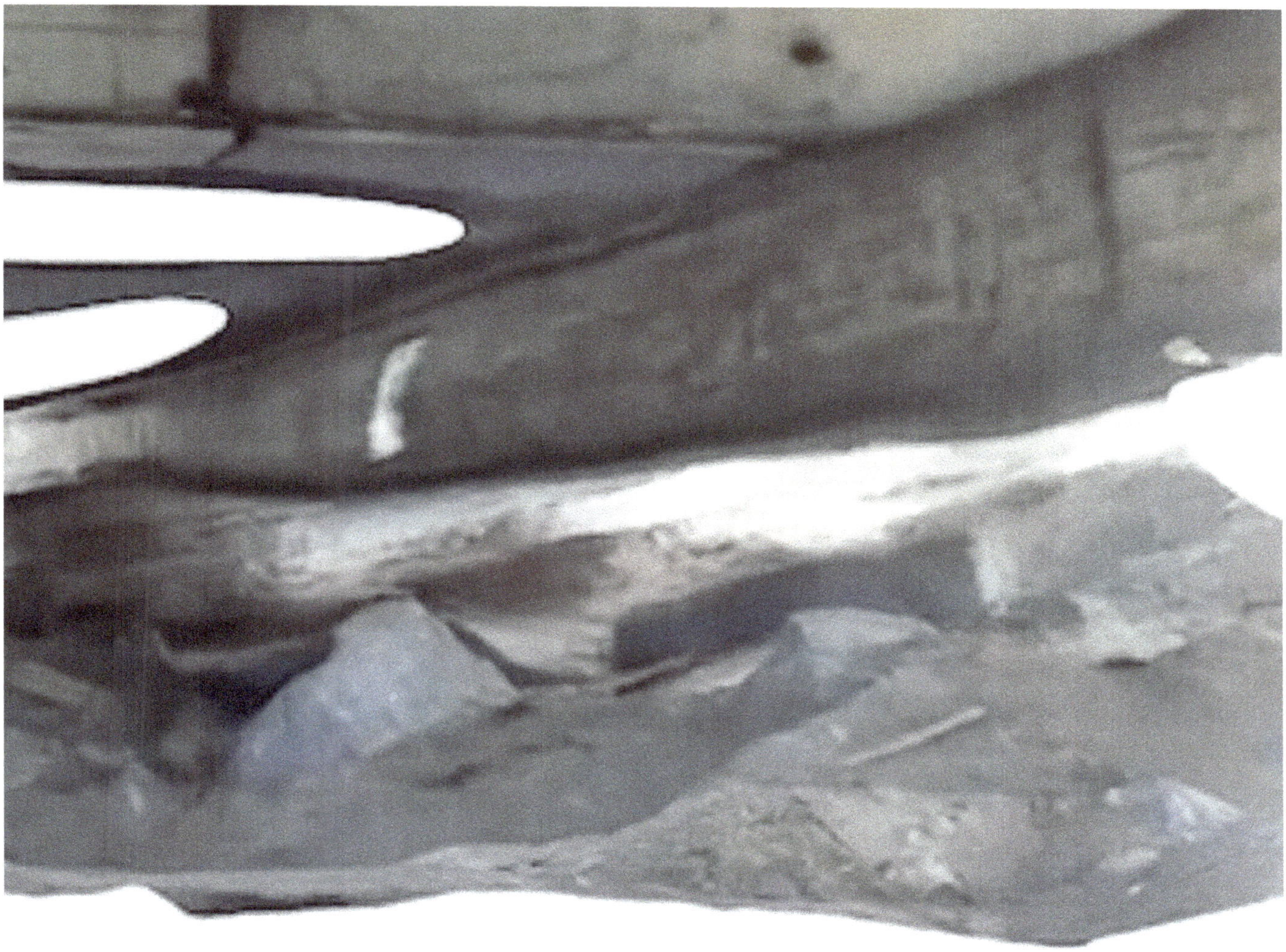

4. DIGITAL MODEL

4. DIGITAL MODEL

4. DIGITAL MODEL

MOVING
materials and ways of life

Essay by James Benedict Brown

MOVING

On a small bluff, a few kilometres from where I'm writing this, stands a bright yellow farmhouse. Framed by two large red barns, home to forty head of cattle and a workshop that can be used to fix anything from fuse to a forklift truck, the timber house sits on a foundation of large granite blocks. Clad in bright yellow painted timber, the house has stood there for more than one hundred and twenty years, overlooking broad valleys to the east and west. It is one of the oldest houses in the vicinity, but it started its life some 40km to the west. In the late nineteenth century, when inland travel was easier in the winter, it was moved to its current location. The house was disassembled and its component parts stacked on horse-drawn sleds. Its owners had realised that there would be better opportunities for them to farm the land elsewhere. So, the house would be moved. Although absurd to outsiders, the process of moving houses (husflyttningar) in northern Sweden is quite common. A husflyttning will always draw a crowd of spectators and perhaps get a photograph in the local newspaper, but what is most remarkable about the act of moving a house is how unremarkable it is.

Historically, it was more common for timber houses to be disassembled, moved in carefully numbered pieces like the farmhouse described above, and reassembled on a new site. Houses have been moved in Sweden for as long as houses have been built. When southern Scandinavian people started to colonise the north of Norway and Sweden, they did so in pursuit of trading relationships with the south. Whereas the indigenous Sámi peoples derived their living directly from the land and sea, southerners' survival in the north was always framed by economic relationships with the south. Therefore, the southern Swedish relationship to the north has always been defined by an economic pragmatism:

the forest is a resource to be harvested, the ground contains minerals to be mined. If a resource exists, a community will flourish to harvest it. If a resource is depleted or no longer economically viable, that community will inevitably diminish and disappear.

Whereas contemporary timber houses in Sweden are typically of frame construction, the oldest buildings are made of solid wood. Trees are felled and trunks are planed into pieces that are laid horizontally on top of one another. These beams are held together by tabs and grooves cut into the top and bottom. Wooden pegs or steel nails brace pieces together, contributing to a naturally sturdy and well insulated interior. Moving such a building was a matter of disassembling it and numbering the components so that they could be re-assembled in correct order. With the availability of vehicles powered by fossil-fuels, the possibility of moving a house in its entirety became conceivable.

So unimaginably vast were the forests of northern Sweden that the first Scandinavians to cut down trees for industrial purposes did so with no consideration for replanting. It was simply assumed that northern Sweden was so large that there would be enough raw material for a continuous wave of extraction. The 2022 decision of the Swedish Ministry of Enterprise, Energy and Communications to allow a British company to start mining for iron ore in Kallak (Gállok in Sámi) represents the culmination of more than a century colonial pragmatism: the material exists; therefore, it should be extracted, irrespective of the harm to the environment or indigenous communities.

The first southerners who settled in the north cut down trees to clear land for agriculture, to build houses and to provide fuel. But if a place failed to be economically viable for settlement, so a house might move somewhere else. Today, the well documented depopulation of rural Sweden prompts dogmatic approaches to the built environment. Although constructing and operating buildings contributes approximately one third of all carbon emissions in Europe, the demolition of surplus housing occurs often. In 2021, municipal councils in the towns of Dorotea and Vilhelmina agreed independently of one another to demolish three large and serviceable blocks of apartments.

Their useful economic lives were over, since it would be more expensive to keep them than to demolish them. Built of masonry and concrete, the ends of their useful lives were in fact determined by their very immobility.

This material dimension is important. Whereas low-lying Denmark is naturally rich in clay and a consequent expertise in building in brick, Sweden is densely forested. The abundance of wood has contributed to a rich culture of building with wood. Timber is also a more forgiving material, one that allows the untrained builder plenty of leniency. Wood buildings are flexible, fitting together in a way that allows for movement over time, as the dead load of the building, the live loads of its inhabitants, precipitation and wind act on it. Wooden buildings tolerate to no small degree twisting, flexing and racking.

This movement, both in the flexing of a building over time and in the movement of entire buildings from place to place, is contradictory to many of our cultural assumptions about housing. In most of the Romantic languages, the word for real estate is derived from some variant of immobilier (French), imobiliária (Portuguese) or immobiliare (Italian). The house is imagined as something that is immobile, and therefore worthy of a particular financial status. In northern Sweden, however, houses are moved so routinely that the economic questions are distilled to an almost asinine simplicity. Buildings have also been relocated for cultural reasons. With industrialisation in the late nineteenth century came a realisation that ways of living and working were being lost. In both Norway and Sweden, this led to the establishment of a number of open-ar museums to preserve built culture. In Oslo, the librarian and historian Hans Aall (1869–1946) established the Norsk Folkemuseum (Norwegian Folk Museum) in 1894, now home to a variety of buildings brought to Oslo from the different regions of the country. This includes the famous Gol Stave Church, built in the late twelfth century, which was saved by the Society for the Preservation of Ancient Norwegian Monuments (Fortidsminneforeningen) when a new church was proposed in 1880. In Sweden, the open-air museum Skansen was established in 1891 by Artur Hazelius (1833 - 1901). Hazelius, like Aall, was a folklorist concerned with the preservation of ways of life that were threatened by Scandinavia's rapid modernisation. He raised funds and established collections of objects, including buildings, as a record of what was regarded as the traditional way of Swedish life.

On the website of one Swedish company that moves houses is the assertion that 'whether it is possible or not to move a house is usually a question of whether the house is worth more than the cost of moving it.'

Inspired by Skansen, the Västerbottens Museum and adjacent open-air park Gammlia were established in Umeå in 1921. Gammlia established a collection of objects and buildings which represented the pre-industrial history of northern Sweden, albeit one that at first prioritised a southern and non-indigenous culture. The first building moved to Gammlia was a manor house from Sävar, built in 1806. Moved in 1921, it took 132 horse-drawn loads to bring the house in pieces to Gammlia.

A gatehouse from Bureå followed later in 1921, as well as a small cottage from Jämteböle in Vännäs. In 1955, a chapel built in 1802 on the island of Holmön that had been deconsecrated sixty years previously (and variously used for doing laundry and keeping livestock) was also moved.

Today, the open-air museums in Oslo, Stockholm and Umeå have used the relocation of houses and other culturally significant buildings to assemble and present an edited history of not only our built environment, but also our cultural environment. But like in any museum, the buildings risk reification: they become static objects removed from the context in which they were conceived. The ease with which these buildings were moved suggests that in Scandinavia there might exist another intellectual approach to understanding architectural context. As the iron ore mine at Kiruna, the largest in the world, has gradually expanded and undermined the city that services it, there has been a typically pragmatic approach to the problem: the city must be moved.

Understanding these movements, whether for economic or cultural purposes, and whether piecemeal or wholesale, gives us an opportunity to understand some of the fundamental intellectual questions about our built environment.

It may only be a house, and it may only draw a small crowd, but every husflyttning is an opportunity to see inside, underneath and in between the assumptions about that which is supposedly immobile.

Dahlgren, M. (2021) 'Dom: Beslut om rivning av hyreshus inte olagligt.' Västerbottens Kuriren [Online], 1 May. Retrieved from: https://www.vk.se/2021-05-01/dom-beslut-om-rivning-av-hyreshus-inte-olagligt

Johansson, J. (2021) 'Hyreshusrivningar i Dorotea blev dyrare än förväntat.' Västerbottens Kuriren [Online], 15 December. Retrieved from: https://www.vk.se/2021-12-15/hyreshusrivningar-i-dorotea-blev-dyrare-an-forvantat

MOVING

MOVING

MOVING

MOVING

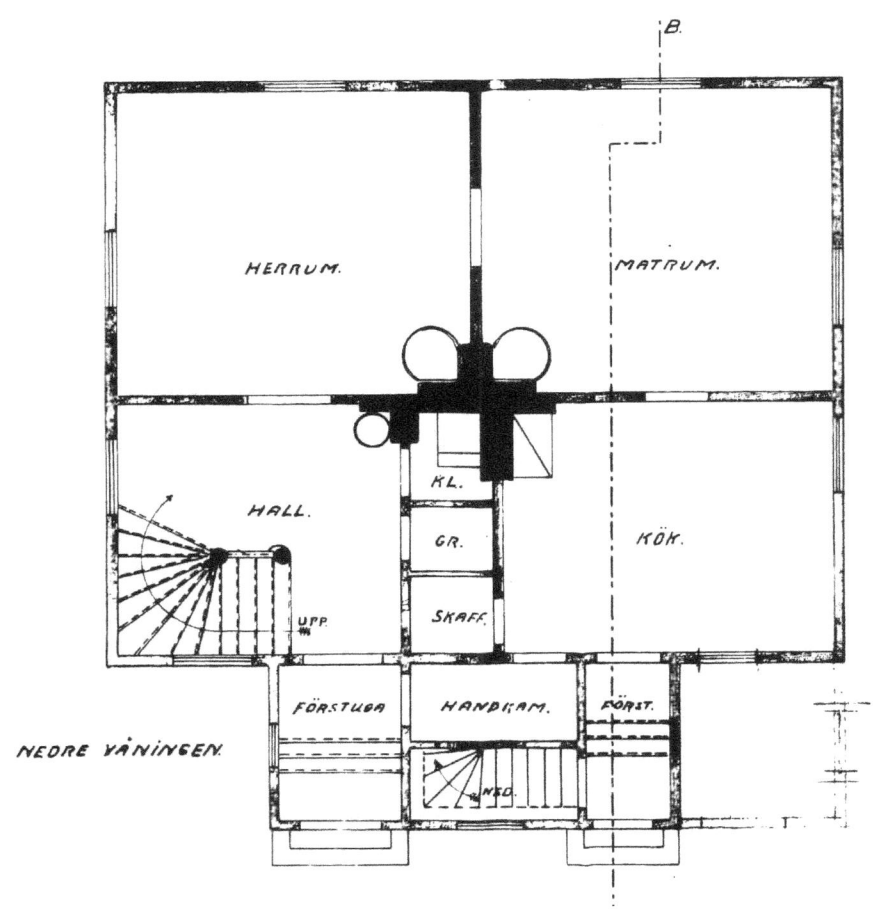

MOVING

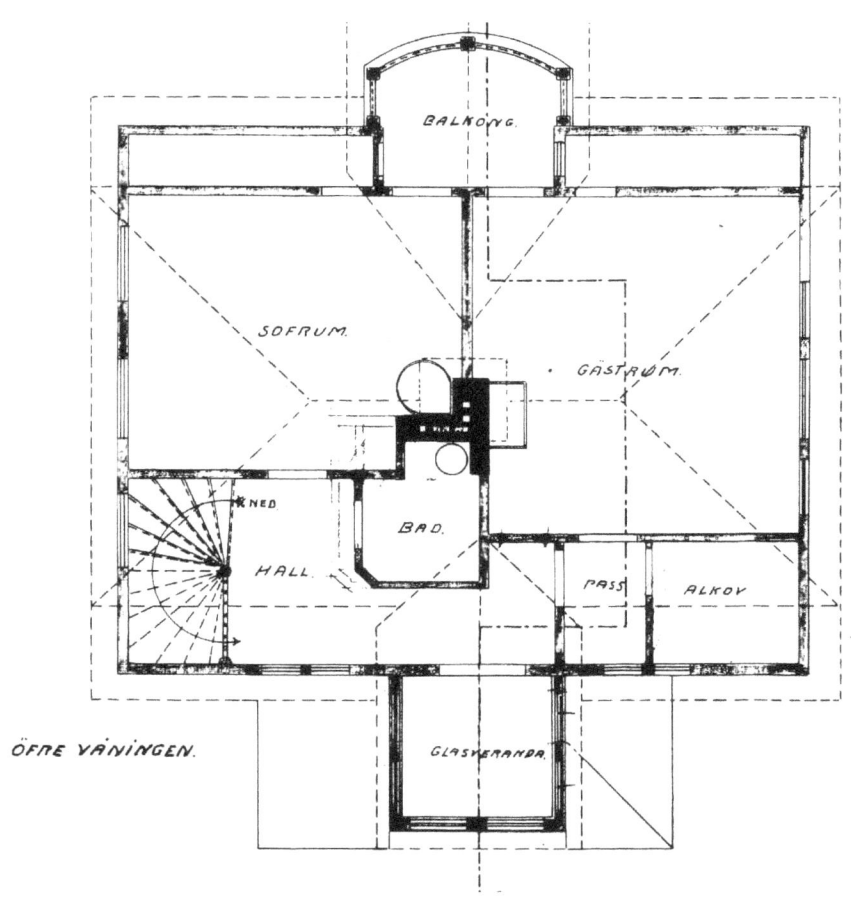

MOVING

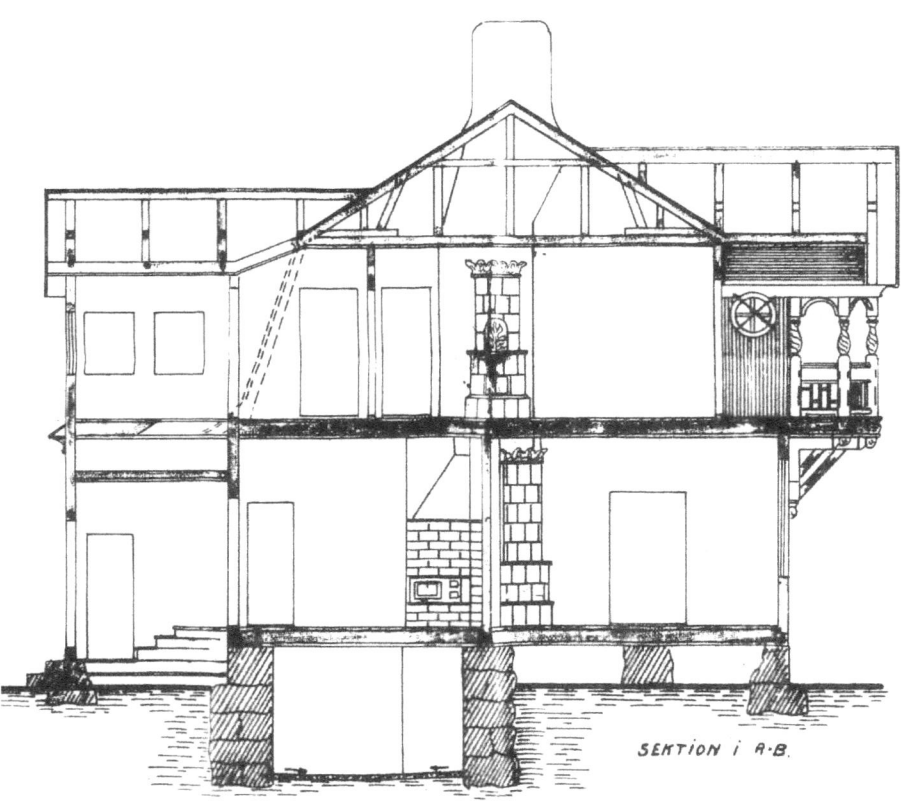

SEKTION I A-B.

MOVING

A HOUSE MOVED
[Husflyttningar]

A written and visual essay by Tonia Carless + Robin Serjeant

MOVED

This essay formed the basis of a projected presentation to a staff research seminar at the School of Architecture UMA Umeå University in February 2022. The seminar was held outside in the forest at the Eastern edge of Lake Nydala, which currently forms the Eastern edge of the city of Umeå. The seminar involved a reading, a local audience and a digitally distant audience (via the platform zoom). It was a reading and series of projected collage works from the research project and the moving house onto one of the cabins at Nydala Lake, due for demolition as part of the ongoing gentrification of the area and city.

The seminar was planned for projection onto the wall of the cabin at 16.30, in darkness and in sub zero temperatures (-12) using a battery-operated projector and laptop, smartphone and retrieved furniture from the cabin. Shortly before the seminar was due to start the demolition bulldozer moved onto the site to shift a pile of gravel (the mound) to make a pathway for the demolition works. The projection was relocated to an adjacent outbuilding store that formed part of the collected cabins [stuga] on the site and the demolition continued during the first part of the presentation. Discussion continued in and around the demolition and forest site.

This event was understood to be a layering of images from the moving house to another site and surface of gentrification and economic and social change, to establish a material, spatial, social discourse. The active participation and live performance in the space was also understood to recognize the limitations of academic research and practice within the confines of the university ascribed spaces. (See the presentation slides)

This will consider the research output from a collaborative, interdisciplinary, practice-based research centred on moving residential buildings in Umeå, Västerbotten.

This incorporates a visual essay that documents an archival study of moving a house from Teg in Umeå city centre a distance of ten kilometres to the suburban fringes of the city. The house move was made by three men, from Nya Töre Husflyttningar

AB, using traditional techniques, synonymous with northern hemisphere latitudes. The move required legal and administrative permissions, covering the movements of things and bodies across the landscape. It was carefully documented as a process from April-December 2021, with the low-loader transportation happening over 6 hours on Midsummer evening from 20:00. It was probably the largest public gathering seen in Umeå city centre during the time of isolating recommendations associated with the Covid pandemic. The feat of moving houses is a familiar event in the region. This building is particular and special to this part of the city due to its status as historic villa.

The focus for the research has been the space beneath the building, between land and occupation. It is understood to represent more than the increasing land values that have precipitated its move. It is a space through which to consider the material, social, political, economic and legal frameworks which construct ideas of Norrland. The space is an initial repository for this project for representation, participatory and performative architectures. These questions will be considered further by making an object that captures the space beneath a building to be moved, to question also the process of moving the buildings. It will investigate how the buildings and spaces change when the building is moved and installed at another place.

The object for research is centred on what was known and not known about those spaces, and what are the social, cultural and economic factors that helped shape what was known.

This session has 'after the move' as a departure point and showed a short film of a midwinter event of projecting images through the empty house. It was conceived as a work in progress to develop associations and ideas towards a physical model of the space under the house.

The projections are always to consider the multiple layers of knowledge and histories formed from the moving action, and to ask: what is moved? The project is not motivated by nostalgia but by questions and insights around this context. The justification made to Umeå Kommun for making the historic house move was that Teg, its original site, was a rural area when the house was built in the 1910's and that it would be more appropriate, in terms of historic context then to return it to a rural location. The proposal was made by the current owner, a third generation of a family that cared for the house. This particular move indicates a form, ground and economies of both technological and social change and gives insight into the future formation and configuration of space of the city. The land is due for development as a multi storey city apartment block, part of continuing speculative investment in the form of acquisition and development of land assets.

The particularity of this project is directed at a concrete understanding of some of the industries and practices of architecture production. The practices of land speculation, conversion of rural land to settlement, material specifications, and building technologies are part of increasing applications of neoliberal economy in the region. The project is also seen as offering an understanding of how the transformation of the Swedish Nation state from the project of making of an egalitarian society has been distorted by globalisation and the neoliberal agenda, as buildings can all be moved to form other potentially more productive spaces. The neo-liberal agenda here is taken to be the imposition of what are understood to be market forces in the provision of public services and ownership/control of supply over things held in common.

The project considers the state apparatus (physical and legal infrastructure) required for the transportation and control of buildings and substances (earth, logs, minerals, snow, roads) to investigate wider questions of who owns Umeå? What are the political narratives embedded in physical space? The proposition is that there are multiple, sometimes simultaneous constructions of culture, of history, heritage, and forms of spatial occupation and that all of these layers can be found in Västerbotten and throughout Norrland.

This is the production of another social-spatial understanding of the lived environment of Norrland in contradistinction to that being made through market forces. This connects to some of the histories of land appropriations and reclamation in the region. These include the misguided and desperate struggle by the inhabitants of Norrlands to provide a living from the land for themselves and their families, and the appropriation of space for institutions, such as the University of Umeå.

David Loeffler develops a reading through archaeology of contested landscapes and territory and notes that:
The "establishment of the various types of Cottages by the State on some of the most miserable acreage imaginable was accompanied by a flood of national romantic propaganda expounding the virtues of this enterprise. Seemingly divorced from reality, we are told how "Ditch digging is tough but beneficial work..." and that the removal of stones and boulders is not only "...pleasurable labour..." but under certain circumstances also a healthy and exciting game (quoted in Stavenow-Hidemark 1967:68). The economic viability of these homesteads was based on over optimistic expectations and unrealistic estimations on the part of the Government.[1] Most of these farms collapsed within a single life time. The institutionalised loneliness and deprivation of this existence has left behind a bitterness that lives on."

The process of house moving and intensive manual labour is understood here to be precisely in relation to the historic and romantic construction of pleasurable labour.

There are other, much older occupations and forms of knowledge that must be acknowledged, at the least:

Futhermore, the capital investments in Umeå property precipitated the removal of one of the few remaining significant historic villas from the city centre and, notably for the area, one which was aligned to the historic development of land patterns outside and beyond the contemporary urban development grid. The research looks at the interrelation of economic and political frameworks for this process. The small retained buildings, and belongings and artefacts might also be understood to provide evidence of the value of attachment to the wider conception of space in the context of the moving house. How was the life arranged around land divisions, and its location to roads, rivers, when first proposed as new building in 1912? What was displaced in the spatial and ownership model of the small farm/homesteading economy?

The project is made of documenting locations, interventions by way of light projections, publication, and the production of a model. The last part of the project is a proposal for an action to transport and relocate particular findings of this idea, using the mechanism of Husflyttningar.

When traditional timber houses burn down, often the chimney is all that remains.

What is broken/left damaged, left behind from the former occupation of house and garden at Teg?

What is the state of the ground?

The film shown is one of a series of projections from the event and is made around the centre of the house where the stone chimney has been removed, in order to lighten the seventy- tonne load for the move. The fracture that resulted in this void is at the core of the house. The void was the location of heating systems and devices. The film projects onto the inside of the house museum exhibits, documents, wallpapers and more. It also shows a digital modelling of the underside of the house.

In considering what is moved at Teg, another proposed projection event was to return the memory of the house to that site, projecting the windows of the house back into place, to develop a dialogue and exchange around the space of the site itself with inhabitants and neighbours. These projections were part of documenting the ten kilometres journey made in the move.

The event was to be a nighttime projection of the windows and their view as the house is currently back onto the site at Teg. There were multiple considerations of how this might be done as a collaborative event and a wider public discourse. The ideas centered on the notion of projecting the views seen from the windows in Degernäs onto the surrounding buildings back at Teg, to return the new rural views back to the city on the facades of the surrounding buildings.

This was to imagine having lived in the house in the city and then seeing a new view out of the window across the rural location and with a different orientation, with for example the sun rising and setting in a different position, from the same window. This projected a new understanding of the context for architecture and its capacity to be of a wider location and site.

The projections were to be a public event for the neighbours in particular, as these people were the ones who attended the house move in mid-summer and those who came out to talk about it, watch it, follow it and to consider its impact and meaning for them and for the city and specific location at the time.

An idea about how to achieve this was resolved as a series of white portable screens at the edges of the site, where the images could be projected to avoid any problems with, for example, projecting into the windows of surrounding buildings. The event has not to date been completed on the grounds that it may have been detrimental to the owner of the house and his capacity to sell the site. The consideration was that it may have bought some controversy to the site in relation to its lost history and space, particularly while the question of the sale of the land was still at issue. The ethical considerations meant that the event was cancelled and only low-level experiments with projections on surfaces of snow were recorded at the site, not as a public event, but as a testing of projection and surface. This moment allowed for a consideration of the cultural significance of the moving of buildings in the region. The moving was seen as an exciting public event, out of the ordinary, not necessarily because it was a whole building moved in one piece, but because of the historic nature and quality of the architecture, as local and regional heritage piece of the National Romantic style of the era . The moving of buildings is seen more as a regular and frequent occurrence in the region with particular reference to Kiruna, the town that was moved in its entirety, due to mine expansion works and which was undertaken by the mine company LKAB.[3] In considering why this projection might be done it is about what the house move means, both for the occupants of the house and the notion of its histories and the lived experience of the site and the house itself. It asks, what does it mean to wake up in a bedroom, to stand and look out at a view and to have that view changed and displaced. The changed orientation of the house, sunrise and set and light qualities in relation of the interior of the rooms develops an entirely new architecture of form, context and occupation. The gap appearing in the centre of the house at the removal of the chimney also has an impact on perception and understanding of the space because it makes it possible at some time in this moving process to see across the centre of the house from one room to another and even out and beyond across and to the views through the windows. How does the sun fall through and into the house and how does it fall across from one room to another now that the chimney has gone? How does this gap reconfigure how the spaces are experienced?

What does all of this mean for ideas of displacement, dwelling and the regional context?

When will the house and its images be removed from google earth? Will that moment of recording its lived residents for public view disappear? Through who and how, or in what form will these memories be retained are all aspects to be considered through the archive of images. This question is considered through the projection of images, both onto the sites and back into the interior of the house, as the midwinter event of returning the digital model of the underside of the house and other images of the house in its previous contexts and configurations. How does the division of land from the 1932 maps of Teg and its rural condition sit with this? What does it mean in terms of readings and understanding the impacts and arrangements of global capital? The house move is one small example of a reconfigured and experienced space of this kind. There are multiple histories of this in the region. One aspect of the research is to question this practice and to plot its relocations through mapping the 400 plus moves of the house mover.

One view out of the window of the house to the North West was originally of an Umeå Kommun social services building, a view of the city and space of the Kommun support structure. After the house relocation the view is one of the Volvo plant, across farmland outskirts and beyond the city and across the newly formed earth and housing of Degernäs' newly built houses and plots further down the road.

This house move, its spaces and materials, are just one example of a shift which can help to look at and consider more closely the shifting territories of the frontier space of Norrlands, as each move responds to, or is representative of, the economic or environmental pressures of both and of maximizing returns on relocation (Husflyttningar).

The research asks: What does it mean to move house? What kind of radical domesticity and re-inhabitation is formed from the move? How can these aspects be formed into a reading of the space is a question which is central to the project, in the hope that it might offer new understandings and a discourse on the future social and environmental impact of global capital and reconfiguration of the region.

The approach to house relocation in Norrlands is and has been synonymous with ideas of sustainability, of an immediate and direct reuse potential that marks a negation of the value of architectural or urban design professions in their compliance with profit driven capital accumulation. The practice of house moving questions the narrative of growth that so often is presented as the vindication of growth, and explanation of professional ethics. The professional disregard for things, surfaces, objects, built elements and domestic life come ways in which to read the value construction of space in Norrland. Understanding these through the multi layered projections and the knowledge constructed, both in preparation for the event, through dialogue with owner, neighbours and moving house workers and during the event itself through creating new readings of the spatial programmes and histories. The land beneath the house move, its processes and fragments could also been seen to be emblematic of the ongoing process of state interventions.

The development of Tomtebo in the area of Umeå in the 1980s and 90s saw the beginning of the pollution of the lake Nydala and its environs and a globalization synonymous with mass consumption of landscape for tourism. It was and continues to be stages of market development in a process of further commodifying nature, as part of the internal market colonisation and re-colonisation of northern Sweden.

The cabins at Nydala have a long and significant history of use for recreational purposes with a low density, sustainable approach to the land and its resources. The controversial demolition and repurposing of many of the Nydala lake cabins for the mass, private, developer led appropriations is another example of this form of reconfiguration of space. This seminar was presented from one of these cabins.

The next stage of research proposed is to make a model to consider the negative space under the house as a series of layered materials associated with the process of house building, landscape, resources extraction, sloyd craft practices. The materials specification will include sawdust, iron ore, copper, birch bark and organic matter.

The spaces and form of the model will consider the extending spatial underside of the gap between house and land, and the ten kilometres journey through new developments, such as Ikea and retail, out of town, shopping complex.

The formal development of the model will engage with speed and flows of material. It will also consider ideas of pressing as a point of both accrued and extracted material and matter.

The small prototype model is to be a scale to be transported by EPA* from Umeå in a Northerly direction, an event to attract and engage with a crowd.

*The EPA is a mode of transport used by the youth of Norrlands, in part to undermine the state regulation of freedom to roam for the underage driver. EPA are mechanically and spatially adjusted vehicles, such as Volvo cars that have a maximum speed of thirty kilometres per hour and a maximum passenger capacity of two. They originate from a set of regulations intended to allow young members of farming families to drive heavy farm vehicles and tractors but, through a process of adaptation, have become synonymous with operating at the fringes of state control of traffic movement. It is a practice virtually unrecognised or heard of in the south of Sweden. The EPA driver is also conceived of as a form of 'other', as a point of contesting the freedoms and limitations of moving in the region.

How might these actions be framed as a research process and methodology for figuring territory?

[1] Loeffler, David (2005) Contested Landscapes/ Contested Heritage Phd thesis.
[2] Harvey, David (2011) The Enigma of Capital and the Crisis of Capitalism
[3] Local media coverage April 2021
The mine company LK lab undertook the moving of Kiruna during a period from 2000, in order to continue and expand the process of extraction from the site. The town buildings including housing and a significant church and community building had been in location since the mine was started in 1898. The context for this and the publicity around it are understood to be significant to include as a thinking about the space underneath and between building and land here for the model.

MOVED

MOVED

MOVED

MOVED

MOVED

5. MOVING INSIDE DAGERNÄS

5. MOVING INSIDE DEGERNÄS

A light installation in the interior of the house in Degernäs.

5. MOVING INSIDE DAGERNÄS

The demolished chimney left a vertical hollow through the heart of the house, with a sense of its rupture and opening up to the harsh winter elements from above. With permission from the owner, Anders Hallstrom, a group of architecture students and researchers set up a light installation in the interior of the house in Degernäs, to further develop projected layers of images and film from the moving and moved house.

These images included historic maps, architectural drawings, the digital model and historic photographs and surfaces from The Västerbotten Museum in Umeå.

The Light projections were conceived of as a small vision event to reinstate occupation through light, shadow and movement, using the Northern Swedish tradition of illuminated windows in the darkness of a long midwinter day with its minimal daylight hours. Light projections centred on the different windows and the hollow of the ruptured chimney. The views from the surroundings of the site in Teg were returned as a memory of its previous location.

5. MOVING INSIDE DAGERNÄS

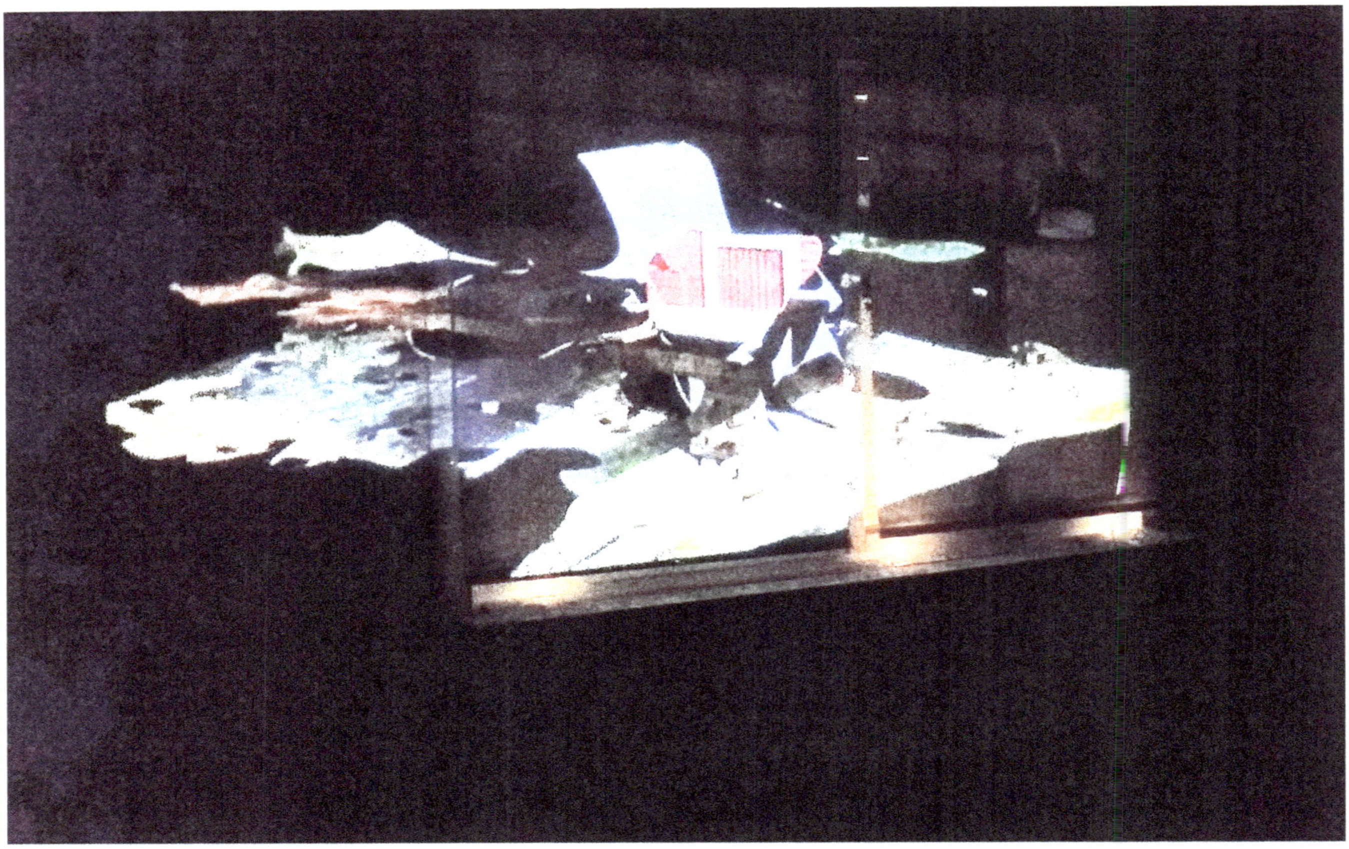

5. MOVING INSIDE DAGERNÄS

5. MOVING INSIDE DAGERNÄS

5. MOVING INSIDE DAGERNÄS

5. MOVING INSIDE DAGERNÄS

5. MOVING INSIDE DAGERNÄS

5. MOVING INSIDE DAGERNÄS

5. MOVING INSIDE DAGERNÄS

5. MOVING INSIDE DAGERNÄS

5. MOVING INSIDE DAGERNÄS

5. MOVING INSIDE DAGERNÄS

5. MOVING INSIDE DAGERNÄS

5. MOVING INSIDE DAGERNÄS

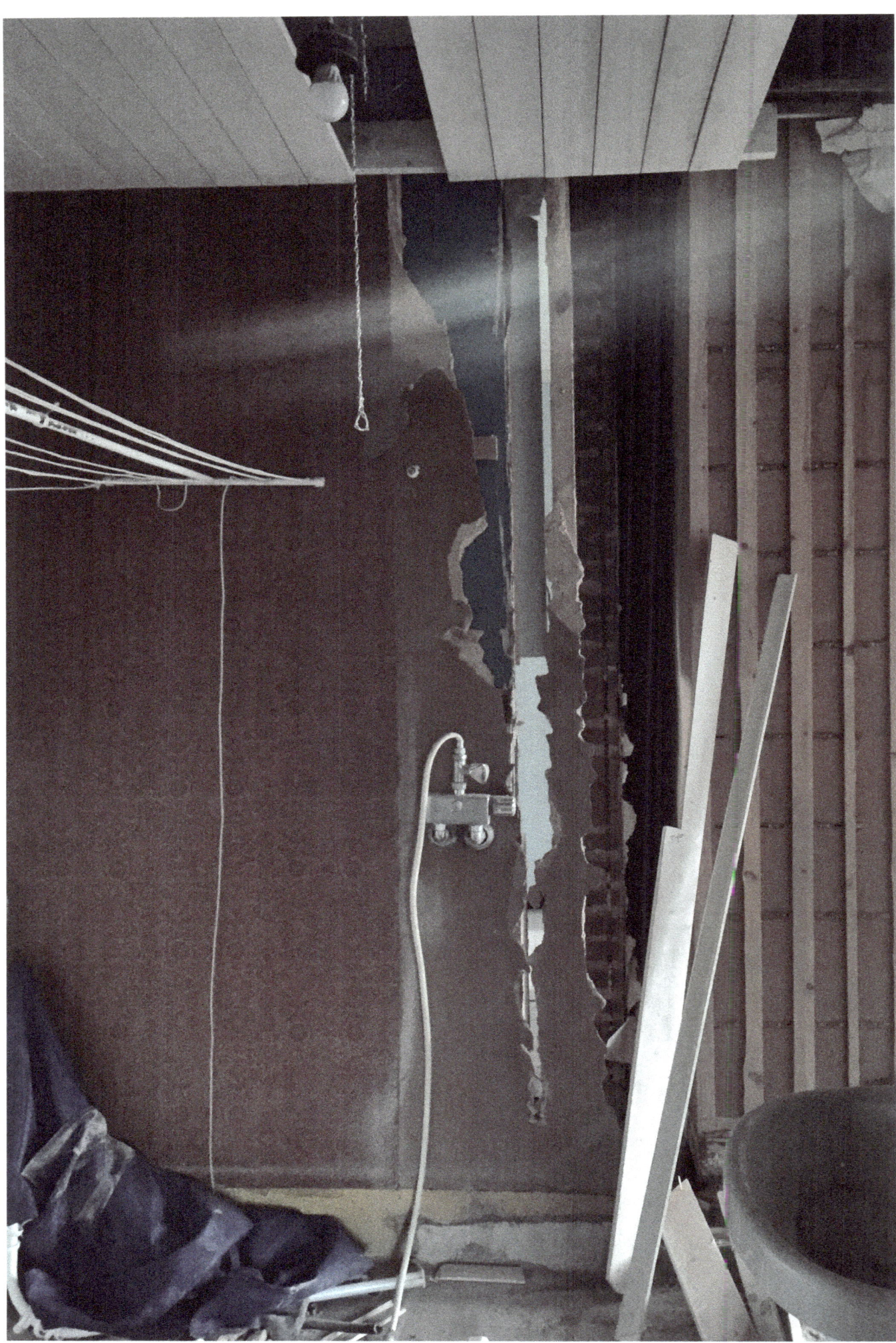

5. MOVING INSIDE DAGERNÄS

5. MOVING INSIDE DAGERNÄS

5. MOVING INSIDE DAGERNÄS

6. LONG LOAD [LÅNG LAST]

6. LONG LOAD [LÅNG LAST]

Returning the house as a projected memory to the site at Teg.

6. LONG LOAD [LÅNG LAST]

The intention of returning the house as a projected memory to the site at Teg is a future event proposal. Some aspects of this were explored through a series of light projections as a small vision event on the move, along the ten kilometres route. This considers both the idea of occupying the house in its new location, of the new views of the rural location, from inside the house, through the windows and the histories of its occupation and relationship with its surrounding garden, city and small outbuildings. It also considers the elements that were moved on route, signs, cables, bus stops and more, and the momentary glimpses of the house emerging across different city and landscapes in the context of a setting midnight sun.

6. LONG LOAD [LÅNG LAST]

6. LONG LOAD [LÅNG LAST]

6. LONG LOAD [LÅNG LAST]

6. LONG LOAD [LÅNG LAST]

6. LONG LOAD [LÅNG LAST]

6. LONG LOAD [LÅNG LAST]

6. LONG LOAD [LÅNG LAST]

6. LONG LOAD [LÅNG LAST]

6. LONG LOAD [LÅNG LAST]

6. LONG LOAD [LÅNG LAST]

6. LONG LOAD [LÅNG LAST]

6. LONG LOAD [LÅNG LAST]

6. LONG LOAD [LÅNG LAST]

6. LONG LOAD [LÅNG LAST]

7. SINKING. OTHER LIVES OF THE CABIN [STUGA] DEMOLITION

7. SINKING. OTHER LIVES OF THE CABIN [STUGA] DEMOLITION

The moving house in relation to the ongoing reconfiguration of dwelling space in and around Umeå.

7. SINKING. OTHER LIVES OF THE CABIN [STUGA] DEMOLITION

This section provides an understanding of the context of the moving house in relation to the ongoing reconfiguration of dwelling space in and around Umeå and especially of values associated with the Nydala Cabins (stuga). It considers how the city is increasingly commodified through removal, demolition and unbuilding. Light projections were made of all the subsequent layers as a small vision event, onto the partly demolished cabins [stuga] at Lake Nydala. This projection considers a conceptual moving of the house into the wider context and developing a framework for understanding it as part of the reconfiguration of space in Västerbotten.

7. SINKING. OTHER LIVES OF THE CABIN [STUGA] DEMOLITION

7. SINKING. OTHER LIVES OF THE CABIN [STUGA] DEMOLITION

7. SINKING. OTHER LIVES OF THE CABIN [STUGA] DEMOLITION

7. SINKING. OTHER LIVES OF THE CABIN [STUGA] DEMOLITION

7. SINKING. OTHER LIVES OF THE CABIN [STUGA] DEMOLITION

7. SINKING. OTHER LIVES OF THE CABIN [STUGA] DEMOLITION

7. SINKING. OTHER LIVES OF THE CABIN [STUGA] DEMOLITION

7. SINKING. OTHER LIVES OF THE CABIN [STUGA] DEMOLITION

7. SINKING. OTHER LIVES OF THE CABIN [STUGA] DEMOLITION

DIALOGUE THREE

Dialogue Three
What is this mound?

A discussion about the
demolition of cabins at
Lake Nydala,
their relation to
the moving house
and a small vision event

Tonia Carless + Robin Serjeant

DIALOGUE THREE

Dialogue 3. What is this mound?
What are the objects leaning against the tree?
Are the leaning trees part of this situation?
these days have been so full and so extreme in many ways. It's a full moon, an Aurora, ice swimming, sledding, trips to the sea and Degernäs and it's quite a lot sometimes in the cold too
the moving house and naming the research I find difficult, so the legal framework is important for this too. I think that the state apparatus required for the transportation (I'm thinking again of all these trucks moving earth, minerals and now snow too) is really important to investigate and the wider question then of who owns Umeå and the political narrative embedded in the physical space of course and more.
For Sweden it is a question of:
How has the transformation of the intention of social equity of the Swedish nation state been distorted by commodification and the neoliberal agenda?
(Matt Hynam's model shows this)
For the project here it is a matter of the production of a new domestic space and social spatial understanding of the lived environment of Norrland. This is the discursive potential of the model, of the underside of the house, transported itself for presentation to the general Swedish population.
List of things achieved so far:
Creation of a photogrammetry digital model — Matt Hynam
Photo Archive of the house move sites and spaces under different times and conditions summer/ winter
Small action event inside and outside house in new site — several participants
Small vision projection in Nydala cabins as part of the research seminar.

brick pillars, (chimney breasts, stacks) perhaps to be a point of rest for the object?

DIALOGUE THREE

when I looked it up it was always about
burning housing earmarked for refugees, but
I don't think that this image was from this,
it's just stock footage and I chose it because
you can see the burned previous structure.
Talking heads 2nd reference 'Burning Down the
House'.
"Oh yes, no visible means of support and you
ain't seen nothin' yet, everything's stuck
together, I don't know what you're expecting
staring into the TV set…
Fighting fire with fire"
your reference to burning down dwellings
around refugee shelter is shocking. And I
remembered the synagogue / Jewish Association
in Umeå closed a year or so ago, because of
racism.
And I think of the land settlement /
reclamation - the ditch digging, and idea
of claiming and taming the land, through
smallholdings, which could lead to — a Wild
West, This is my land, won and protected by my
and my family's labours.... blood and soil and
fir tree ideas?
Perhaps lidar scan of object in different
locations/situations?
It would have been brilliant to have him scan
the house moving / cabin / sawdust house
demolition.
One research thought: what relation does the
contemporary stuga in Norrlands have to the
idea of enclosure in England? Stuga / cottage
before the enclosures act the cottages was
a labourer with land. After the enclosures
act the cottager was a farm labourer without
land. Finland, Swedish 'Stuga' a residential
building that is used as a holiday or free
time dwelling and is permanently constructed
or erected on its site (statistics Finland
wiki) … where is the free time?

The seminar might start with setting

DIALOGUE THREE

principles eg - degrowth, uncertainties of
what is known / how things known, immediacy,
other directions and orientations......in
context of capitalist systems (David Harvey)

Summary points on right to roam.
I was thinking about the image that was
sliding off the side of the bath as a format
for the next projections (of vertical moving
into horizontal) or a slope towards the zoom
audience.

https://www.theguardian.com/world/video/2022/jan/25/life-in-the-arctic-the-reindeer-herders-struggling-against-the-climate-crisis

This is Teg of course. The rupture and wrench.
And the bins left behind.
The confetti of the paper left behind - stamps
and torn wallpaper(?).
Long winter tree outline shadows over fields
and hedges. I am taken with these appearances,
after so long in the city.
I also know that the invisible matter
- policy, corporate profiteering around
landownership / chemicals industry, the
subjugation and marginalisation natural
systems (habitat loss, reproduction numbers
dropping, pollutants) and subjugation and
marshalling of animals as direct and indirect
food units, make these very troubling scenes,
in English midlands and north.
The essay by Wendell Berry
Problem: what model could be more visually
arresting than this
 what we need to make in addition to the
collage is a map which shows all the houses
that moved from and in Umeå, including those
demolished. This should be made through the
sloyd practice of pressing/embossing, like
timber baulks into soft wet ground
The blizzard is still dangerous I think to
travel too far

DIALOGUE THREE

city eating itself

list for leaving house with for seminar.
New laptop
Projector
HDMI cable
New mobile phone
Power bank for phone.
Charging cable for phone
Charging cable for projector if it can be plugged into power bank (probably not needed)

photo seminar practice set up & seminar in action – giving seminar, lake track
      I am bringing my laptop/ tablet.
Mobile phone and camera (to photo event if possible)
Bus ticket....

cast metal landscape)
projection, Matt Hynam cabin.
Well I like it's trajectory
Section
And implications
I sent Elvy Persson a photo of the demolished house and she said "easy to demolish not so easy to build up houses and relations! "

photos historic maps and collages
      I am setting out drawing of the underside of the house…..and looking at photos of the collage laid out on floor.

it's more work in Matta –Clark's
Anarchitectural parade
Umeå the NON-umental city with its moving houses and snow piles

      I think it is something about sinking, settling and uplift (wrenching) which can be developed through Sloyd and other modelling processes of accretion and removal. This is both Husflyttningar and demolition and the

DIALOGUE THREE

recycling sorting piles of the cabins in demolition. Value of the space under the house again
Of baulks pressing and moisture extraction, or moisture extraction from the water course as the land uplifts, or slow growing birches of ancient forests and density of timber of durational working knowledges of structure and load over time that cannot be easily replicated.

Elvy Persson :
"No problem to demolish,
Much harder to build up.
Houses and relations "
And I know …as much as anything can be known … that forming new knowledge like this has to be practice based. It resonates with the first strangeness of the garden of Amir's place and what we came to discover landing here, by being here, by moving from England and what it is to be of this space and as global capital creeps upon it
And the idea that things are knowable, measurable (the technocratic project of Swedish state/culture) falls down on 2 grounds. 1. It is not known what is unknown, and can't be guessed at, no need to guess at – unknowns such as social and cultural formations and phenomena, substances actual not abstracted as quantities and qualities through drawing and digital mapping.
2. How do you propose creative acts? If you don't have that as a motivation, How can you make analyses, and never make things as ways through which to change and develop what you know.

It's not an open ended investigation into: known and what might be unknown.
Its looking at specific moments and phenomena – the particular
Photos of information board, reclaimed park landscape

DIALOGUE THREE

drawing early state all solid
War is really happening in Ukraine

https://www.google.co.uk/search?q=mariele+neudecker&client=safari&hl=en-gb&prmd=inv&source=lnms&tbm=isch&sa=X&ved=2ahUKEwjD1K-jwp72AhVjpIsKHae1BKQQAUoAXoECAIQAQ&biw=375&bih=548&dpr=2#imgrc=say3DQVPhHiGlM

sketch of the underside of the house space
thin panels hung from a frame, with below the baulks stacked up.

The baulks might be timbers, or a cast of the ends of baulks, arranged like photo.

what the model might look like.
should there be a frame that supports panels of material that are made into shapes of the underside?
Under that a stack of timbers?
I think it's more solid, there should be a solid mass which is taken away in part and then added to in other parts

I have been wondering about the surface of a baulk with a photo cut into it

what was on the panels
At the country park
And heaps

information panels, installed at a land reclamation scheme

Matta-Clark's Anarchitecture parade, the model and in fact the house move is/was too. It's explicit at this moment (model and moving) of how global capital moves and consumes the city.

As a moment to contest through close examination

DIALOGUE THREE

resonant in several ways - not just Ukraine, but the internal and external immigration to Norrland, and politics of that movement of bodies.

The problem with the model is one of scale. There is an ambition to
Replicate the spectacle as an event, which is about an improbable thing and load moving through the everyday landscape and the knowledges and histories contained within it. We are currently operating at a very small scale (to be able to
post it as a small casket type thing.) This smaller scale is where we are considering 'what is quality in relation to
touch?' Magnus Wink and the gap between these two scales is a problem to consider EPA size and miniature size
Though I really would like to print out your drawing now at 1:1 and perhaps make the collage to fit somewhere.

sloyd and sketch

What are the dimensions of the house please?
Pallet size 120x120x220

Long elevation balcony / front doors - 10500mm.
Side elevation, staircase side - 8750mm.
Porch side elevation - 2500mm.
Porch frontage - 5870mm.

You probably know, but the shipping container was developed about same time, by an American military engineer. Interesting resonance.
Fish Story, Alan Sekula covers the history of containers i think

DIALOGUE THREE

8. SLOYD MODEL AND OTHER REPRESENTATIONS

8. SLOYD MODEL AND OTHER REPRESENTATIONS

Sloyd, Swedish material craft practice.

8. SLOYD MODEL AND OTHER REPRESENTATIONS

Sinking, settling and uplift developed through sloyd (Swedish material craft practice). Here it is practices of accretion and removal. This section considers different forms of representation of the space beneath the house at Teg. Its initial conception is as a mapping like that of the Tunnumitti – of Greenland with their coastal hand made map which is carved from a piece of timber or bone as a navigational tool to give the coastal outline as a sensational/touch tool to use in a sea fog.[1] Other representations include drawings of the site and its elements, a drawing plotting the underside of the base of the house, collage works plotting the space underneath the house and sketch work towards a larger scale physical model.

[1] Jakobsen, Bjarne Holm. (2000) Kcngelige Danske Topografisk Atlas Grønland Geografiske Selskab Greenland

8. SLOYD MODEL AND OTHER REPRESENTATIONS

8. SLOYD MODEL AND OTHER REPRESENTATIONS

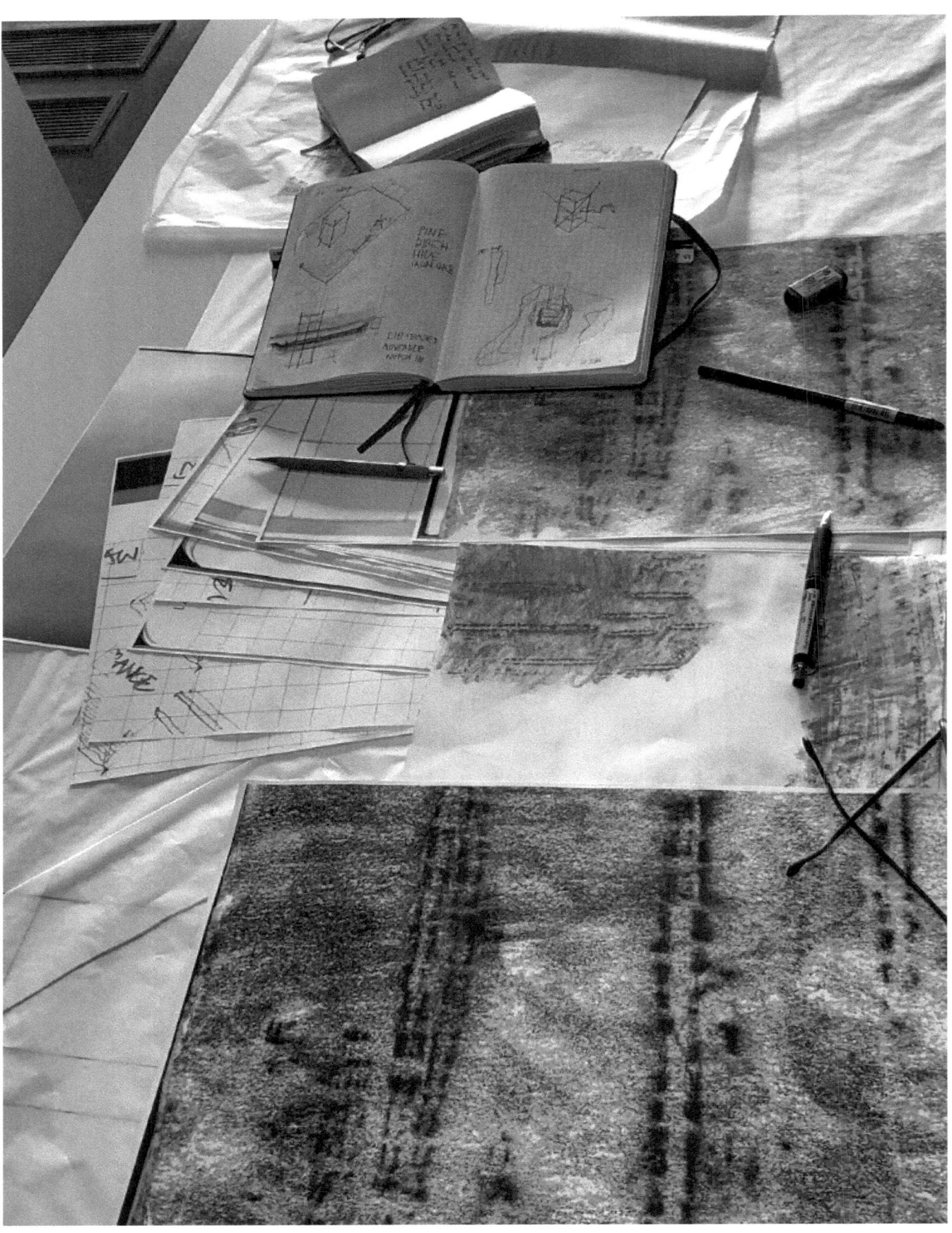

8. SLOYD MODEL AND OTHER REPRESENTATIONS

8. SLOYD MODEL AND OTHER REPRESENTATIONS

8. SLOYD MODEL AND OTHER REPRESENTATIONS

8. SLOYD MODEL AND OTHER REPRESENTATIONS

8. SLOYD MODEL AND OTHER REPRESENTATIONS

8. SLOYD MODEL AND OTHER REPRESENTATIONS

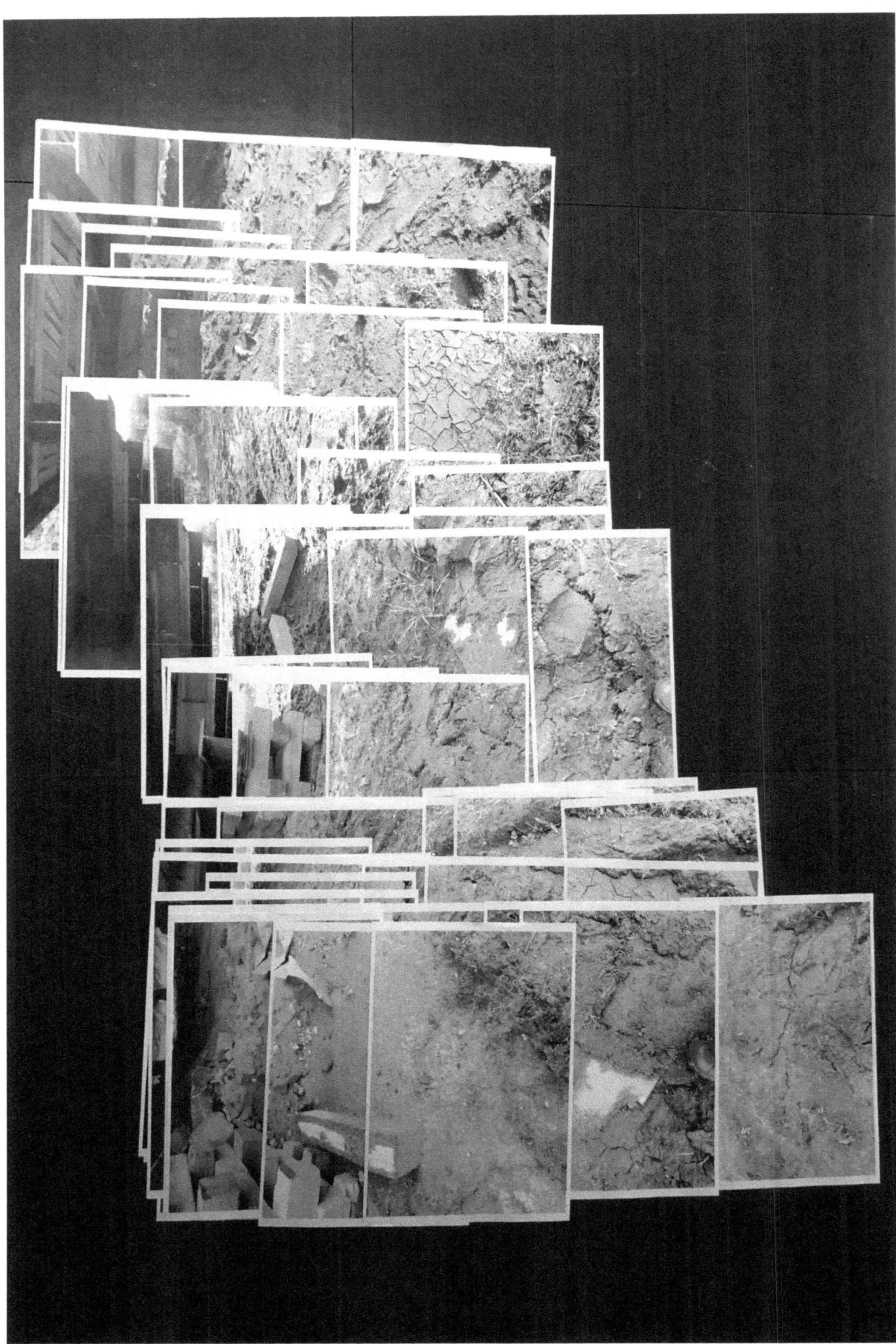

8. SLOYD MODEL AND OTHER REPRESENTATIONS

8. SLOYD MODEL AND OTHER REPRESENTATIONS

8. SLOYD MODEL AND OTHER REPRESENTATIONS

8. SLOYD MODEL AND OTHER REPRESENTATIONS

8. SLOYD MODEL AND OTHER REPRESENTATIONS

8. SLOYD MODEL AND OTHER REPRESENTATIONS

8. SLOYD MODEL AND OTHER REPRESENTATIONS

8. SLOYD MODEL AND OTHER REPRESENTATIONS

8. SLOYD MODEL AND OTHER REPRESENTATIONS

8. SLOYD MODEL AND OTHER REPRESENTATIONS

8. SLOYD MODEL AND OTHER REPRESENTATIONS

8. SLOYD MODEL AND OTHER REPRESENTATIONS

8. SLOYD MODEL AND OTHER REPRESENTATIONS

8. SLOYD MODEL AND OTHER REPRESENTATIONS

8. SLOYD MODEL AND OTHER REPRESENTATIONS

8. SLOYD MODEL AND OTHER REPRESENTATIONS

8. SLOYD MODEL AND OTHER REPRESENTATIONS

8. SLOYD MODEL AND OTHER REPRESENTATIONS

8. SLOYD MODEL AND OTHER REPRESENTATIONS

8. SLOYD MODEL AND OTHER REPRESENTATIONS

8. SLOYD MODEL AND OTHER REPRESENTATIONS

8. SLOYD MODEL AND OTHER REPRESENTATIONS

8. SLOYD MODEL AND OTHER REPRESENTATIONS

8. SLOYD MODEL AND OTHER REPRESENTATIONS

9. HUSFLYTTNINGAR AS CULTURE

9. HUSFLYTTNINGAR AS CULTURE

Husflyttningar as a compressed and conjoined set of terms which implies the action in and of itself.

9. HUSFLYTTNINGAR AS CULTURE

It is hard to fully translate the term husflyttningar directly into English. Moving house implies a change of location for instance and even 'the moving house' is a singular condition of one house moving. Husflyttningar is a compressed and conjoined set of terms which implies the action in and of itself.

This process could be made contextual as a full programme of research thinking, at and of different scales of understanding and relation. On a broad scale it could be a form of response to opensource data on the city and region, as an architecture of degrowth a deterritorialization and even could be reconceived as a moving back in the other direction (back into the city for instance, in this context rather than moving to exploit and profit but as an act of resistance). One project is to understand how perspective changes with movement, for example inside the moved house, looking through the same windows at new and different views.

This particular case of the moving house is framed in part by global capital, but it also has a closer, caretaker history of the three generations of the Hallström family, with the grandfather building the house on a plot where there was also a previous house and then the house being cared for by the father, as a caretaker of its history and the son moving the house as an act of continuing the family tradition and concerns for preserving the history and form of the house as a familial obligation. The movement of the house out to Degernäs and its associated costs, of the move itself, of the land purchase and build up, as well as the cost of full refurbishment to re occupy could only hope to be covered in this particular instance because of the release of potential value of the land beneath the house as prime urban real estate and the potential to maximize returns for the developer purchaser of the land. This is a particular and distinct form of gentrification and simultaneously an economy of extraction. This move also raises the question about what might have happened without such rapid land value increase. Would it have been possible to preserve the house for instance?

In considering the wider context husflyttningar has to be understood as a form of arranging the human condition, not building anew but arriving and departing as a point of architectural urgency and perhaps a response to a society under stress. It is a form of acculturation apportioning value in quite distinct ways. This is in part an economic flow but also one of aesthetic and representational consideration.

It also raises a particular discourse around sustainability and highlights that one of the problems of this term is that of the acceptance of market forces and of ideas of scarcity.
Even if sustainability accepts the fact that road and fuel are not plentiful then an argument for economy of means can still be validated as a once only move of a single resource (the house). In the context of standard construction materials' global price and costs increasing eight-fold, from February 2022 as a consequence of the first few months of the start of war in Ukraine, this argument becomes stronger as environmental, security and political crises intensify. In husflyttningar construction miles are eliminated, so that it is a process which is not

directly productive but rather redistributive and recycled through a very basic set of materials in use, such as timbers, steels and stones.

Sustainability can also be reframed as distribution and allocation of resources or a problem of uneven distribution. The idea that road and fuel are not plentiful constructs, and are scarce can be reconsidered to be an issue only about an even distribution of elements, even in the context of the environmental crisis and this, in turn, can reconfigure how moving buildings are understood in the formation of or resistance to urbanisation

This is a distinct form of de-territo-rialisation, and re-territorialisation. How will this sit in the future forms of digital domain? In this future scheme of uneven development there are already ideas and an acceptance that some people will not have access to real experience, so that cities may only be travelled to and experienced as virtual for example (compounded by poverty of means, pandemics, security instabilities and more). Norrland and husflyttningar in particular offer a precise formation as a resistance to this. The architecture itself has the capacity to explore the real world. It is an on-site solution to construction but has the advantages of being a lighter load and a greater adaptability to circumstance as a reworking of the vernacular of previous civilizations.

An architecture of degrowth here is the idea that to construct contains within it the idea of its undoing and retrieval and that is what is important and explicit. It is also vital as a process of relating to the land and has within it implicit values of mobilisation. There are also implied questions of: Where does it sit, why should it move? Who makes these decisions? To map the series of husflyttningar is to research this and to encircle and enframe the distinct causes of movement and the relations of the space.

It is a physical embodiment of knowledge evidenced through hands and works of Magnus Martensson in this particular case and, as such, can detach from the problems of contemporary mis-information as it is a process of physics and the physical properties of matter, of gravity and a fundamental relation to the earth.

If the soft dimensions of culture make the qualities of place and this stands to some extent as a marker against the idea of modernism, how then can this be read in relation to the culture of husflyttningar? In Norrland it is closely associated with the frontier condition and this emanates from the forest and its timber, with an idea of being beyond or before the church, the state and other institutions. This emerges from a conception of 'free' land for settling. It sits at the heart of temporality and spontaneity.

As a process it amplifies the nomadic, it is also an evidencing of displacement through the process of stressed societies and landscapes (environmentally, economically, and more). In the gathering crowds at Teg on the midsummer evening of 2021 the talk was of the historic house, its specific architectural and historic qualities and merits and a positioning of this in relation to the city as well as its loss as an asset and amenity for the neighbours

9. HUSFLYTTNINGAR AS CULTURE

and locale, as it moved off its original plot. The everyday culture of moving buildings was less spoken, with the implication that moving buildings in itself is not culture but mechanical and structural process which was, none the less, experienced with great excitement.

In the contemporary context of the changing state and spaces of the city of Umeå it might be mobilized to question the reproduction and replication of for example new modernist icons associated with global capital and the spatial reconfiguration of the city.
How do these new architectures rest on the land? How will they replace the existing cultures?
Is it possible to raise the idea of not building as a fundamental approach, to reposition husflyttningar as revolutionary?

9. HUSFLYTTNINGAR AS CULTURE

9. HUSFLYTTNINGAR AS CULTURE

9. HUSFLYTTNINGAR AS CULTURE

9. HUSFLYTTNINGAR AS CULTURE

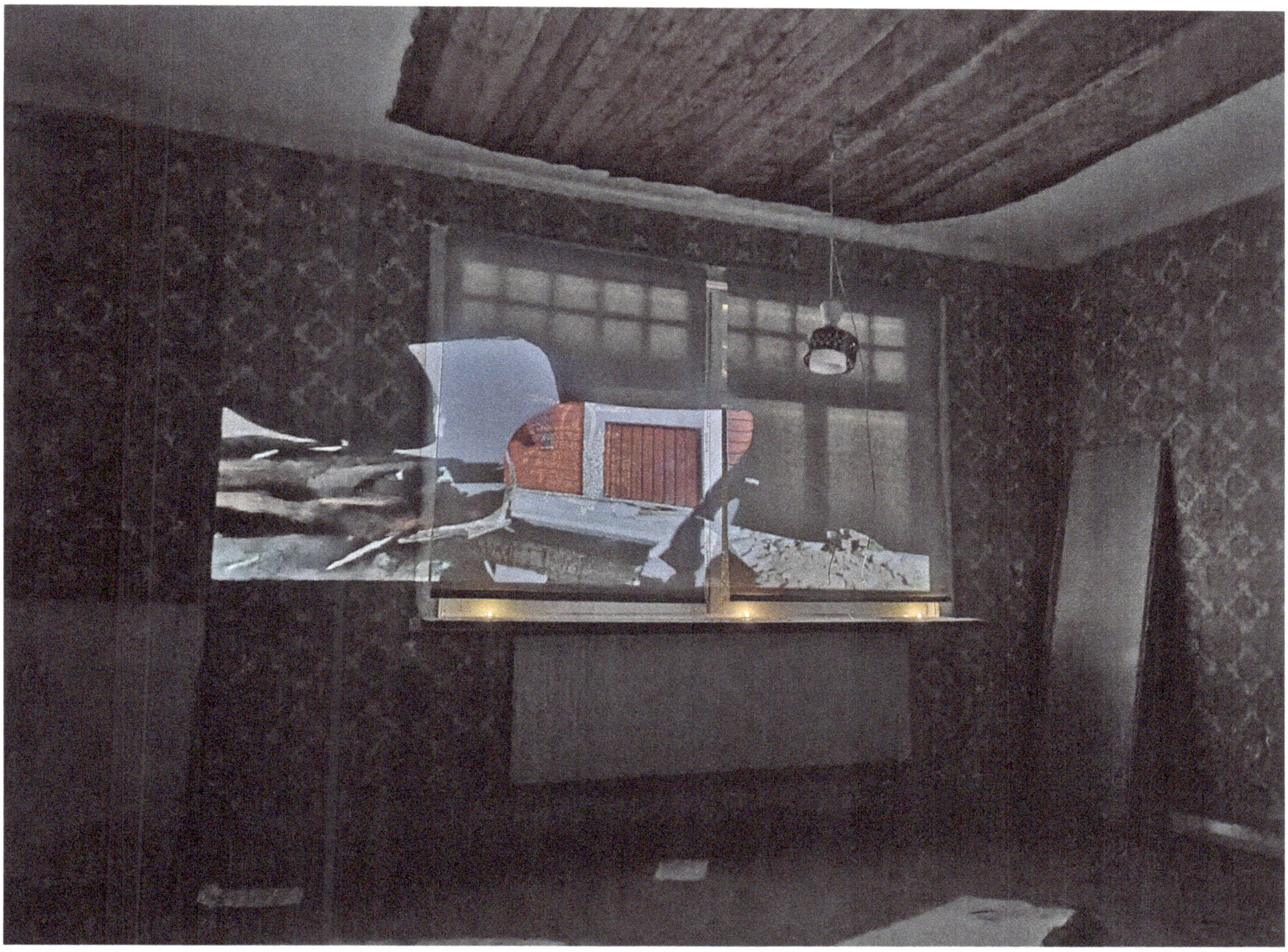

9. HUSFLYTTNINGAR AS CULTURE

9. HUSFLYTTNINGAR AS CULTURE

9. HUSFLYTTNINGAR AS CULTURE

9. HUSFLYTTNINGAR AS CULTURE

9. HUSFLYTTNINGAR AS CULTURE

9. HUSFLYTTNINGAR AS CULTURE

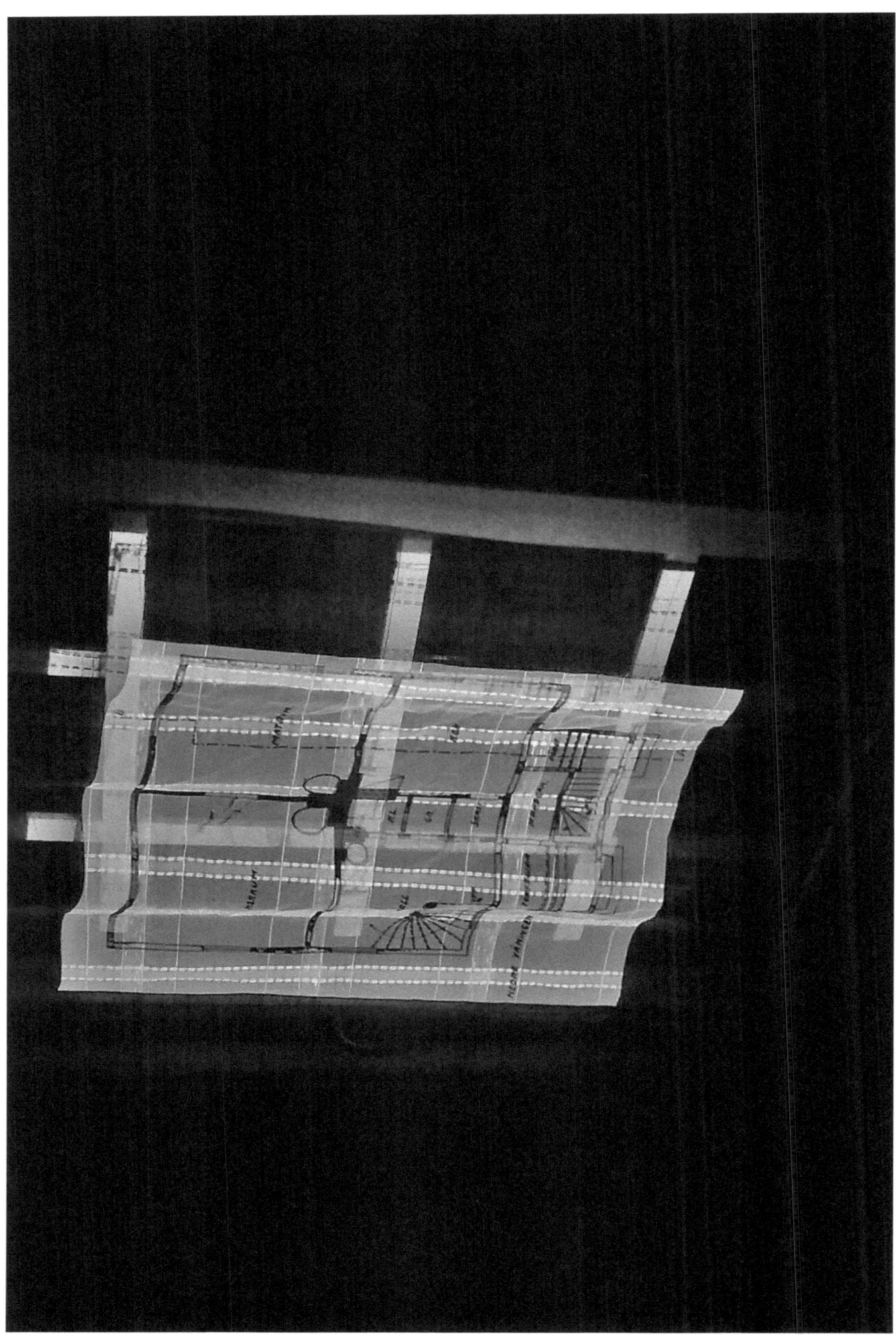

9. HUSFLYTTNINGAR AS CULTURE

EP[A]LOG EVENT

EP[A]LOG EVENT

Proposals for a public event which moves the model as part of a vehicle procession out of Umeå city to the north.

EP[A]LOG EVENT

This section sets out proposals for a public event, installation, performance and exhibition which moves the model as part of a vehicle procession out of Umeå city to the north. It considers the idea of making something strictly functional and ad hoc to stand in for or as a substitute for something else. EPA is the name given to such an object, in this Northern Swedish context specifically making a car into a restricted speed and capacity tractor, but with its origins deriving from a Swedish department store of the same name (Enhetsprisaktiebolaget), with an emphasis that EPA is not about consumer excess but rather functional, modern and available for everyone.[1] Contained within the term is both an idea of rural unsophistication and youth counter culture and mobility.

---

[1] Falk, Pasi and Campbell, Colin. (1997) The Making of A Swedish Department Store Culture. London. Sage Publications pp. 111-136

EP[A]LOG EVENT

MOVING

MOVED

POSTER

a house, moved project.

Volunteers needed for research in action events
Wednesday 1st December & Saturday 4th December 2021
16:00 for 60 to 90 minutes, for one or both sessions

Preliminary action for a research project.

The form of this action: use of light and light projection at two sites in and near Umeå

The research is looking at building, settlement, displacement, substance, reuse and development in the context of *Norrland*

We are asking for assistance with arranging light projections, surfaces, photographing and filming the event and talking about it

Email to Tonia to volunteer by Tuesday 23rd November
tonia.carless@umu.se

A HOUSE MOVED
[HUSFLYTTNINGAR]

ACKNOWLEDGEMENTS

The house moving project was undertaken by Magnus Martensson of Nya Töre Husflyttningar AB who undertook months of work to arrange and move number 9 Lansmansvägen Teg Umeå and who was a generous and patient supporter of the research work and who made the research possible. Magnus is a house mover based in Töre in the far North of Sweden and has physically moved more than 400 buildings. Special thanks also to Erik, who helped work on the move of this house and the lorry driver Albert, both assisting Magnus.

Anders Hallstrom is the owner of the house that moved and very kindly gave access to the interior in November and December 2021 for research, photography and projection and also gave insight into the particular moving process and histories.

Jasjit Singh Senior Lecturer in Industrial Design Lund University, for insight into the house histories and occupation as a near neighbour to the house in Teg.

Elvy and Stina Persson, and Seidi and Abdullah Masalin, local residents and users of Nydala lake and cabins [stuga] for contributions to discussions and thinking, as well as histories on the Nydala cabins and their demolition and understandings about the formations of land, sea and ice in the region as well as their generous social support.

WIDE LOAD
[BRED LAST]

Ingela and Kenneth Hjulfors Berg, their family and friends for their wide-ranging contributions and unparalleled immersive insight into Swedish culture, Umeå Kommun, local social and other landscape insights and who have been central in formulating ideas around the project and in particular their commitment and support in notions of settling in Umeå.

Matthew Hynam, Senior Lecturer in Architectural Thinking, from The University of The West of England School of Architecture, provided a key visual thinking through development of the photogrammetry model in November 2021.

Magnus Wink, Assistant Professor/AMO/International Coordinator Department of Aesthetic Subjects, Umeå University, is central to developing the first stages of the Sloyd model and providing a critical framework for the collaborative making aspect of the project and constructing ideas of quality of making.

Daniel Movilla Vega, Associate Professor of Architecture at UMA School of Architecture, Umeå University, arranged a Staff Research Seminar at UMA School of Architecture, Umeå University, in February 2022, gave a generous space for experimentation and the opportunity to test the small projections from the moving house events to the partly demolished cabins of Nydala, as another research event.

He also provided, together with Mette Harder, a critical creative and supportive framework for thinking through the subject matter and a generous space for pedagogy through their Masters Architecture studio programme Radical Domesticity.

Pia Paulo, Architecture BA student, UMA School of Architecture, Umeå University, August 2020-June 2021 gave insight into the possible exploration and reuse of empty buildings in Västerbotten with an arranged visit to Jörn Railway station and hotel Summer 2021.

James Benedict Brown, Associate Professor of Architecture at UMA School of Architecture, Umeå University, provided the subject matter and location inspiration in Summer 2021, along with enthusiasm and support in film, photography, projection event and critical review essay.

Robin Serjeant, independent architectural educator and researcher, is a joint originator and driver of the research, including all written and visual work .

paula roush, photographer and founder of mobile strategies of display & mediation (msdm), provided editorial support as well as a visual thinking tool in the form of the bookwork.

msdm project in collaboration with Tonia Carless and UWE Bristol (University of the West of England Bristol)/ Interior Architecture 'Studio-Archaelogy provided inspiration for the 3D model of the underside of the house.

This book and research project was part funded by an Umeå University UmArts Small Visionary Project award, with thanks for critical feedback from Ele Carpenter, Anders Lind and Francesco Camilli.

WIDE LOAD
[BRED LAST]

The first iteration is a bookwork
shown at *Relate North 10:
Possible Futures* Symposium
and Exhibition
Yukon University (Yukon School
of Visual Arts)
University of the Arctic's Thematic
Network on Arctic Sustainable
Arts and Design (ASAD),
and the University of Lapland
January 27 & 28 2023

The second iteration is an edition
for the opening of Smedjan
UmArts
Umeå University
Sweden
June 16 & 17 2023

A HOUSE MOVED
[HUSFLYTTNINGAR]

WIDE LOAD
[BRED LAST]

COLOPHON

WIDE LOAD [BRED LAST]
A HOUSE MOVED
[HUSFLYTTNINGAR]

ISBN: 978-1-7391803-1-7

Project by: Tonia Carless

All book section photographs,
Nydala cabin seminar projections
and event arrangement February 2022,
drawings and collage (Sloyd model),
dialogues and research proposal
from inception collaboration:
Robin Serjeant
Tonia Carless

Film and photographs of the moving
house midsummer 21 June 2021
Anna Farnell
James Benedict Brown
Tonia Carless

Digital Model
Matthew Hynam
Sloyd model collaboration
Magnus Wink

EPA Photographs
James Benedit Brown

Film projections, images and
collaborations at the mid winter
small vision event inside at
Degernäs December 2021
Victor Hessner
Sonja Lindgren
Cecilia Tandberg
Emelie Vänman
James Benedict Brown
Robin Serjeant
Tonia Carless

Editorial design collaboration
paula roush
Tonia Carless

Design, layout and bookwork
paula roush

Publication license
Creative Commons
(CC BY-NC-SA 4.0

Published by:
msdm publications

A HOUSE MOVED
[HUSFLYTTNINGAR]

mobile strategies
of display & mediation
msdm.org.uk

WIDE LOAD
[BRED LAST]

A HOUSE MOVED
[HUSFLYTTNINGAR]